Senior Love in Cyberspace

By Susan Alpert and Stephen Morse

Copyright © 2019 Susan Alpert and Stephen Morse

For more infomation contact:
www.susanalpertconsulting.com/senior-love-in-cyberspace.com

ISBN: 978-1-64516-328-2

Printed in the United States of America

Editor: Taylor Holland
Cover and Book Design: Patty King

Senior L♥VE IN Cyberspace

Susan Alpert | Stephen Morse

Table of Contents

Introduction

Senior. Love. Cyberspace.

These three words would undoubtedly be described by my adult children and grandchildren as a triple oxymoron. The same is probably true for many happily married seniors. But when you find yourself suddenly single in your 60s—and on into your 70s—you realize two things: You're never too old for a new love, and online dating really isn't as crazy as it sounds.

This is the story of a man and woman in their mid-70s, separated by the width of a country, but connected by their desire to live a vibrant, compatible, loving life, despite the passage of decades and their aging bodies.

I'll admit, up front, that I am that woman and Stephen is that man. I'll also admit that we met online, something I never would have owned up to a few years ago. I still believed that I shouldn't have to succumb to social media. Magically, Mr. Right would appear in my life, and we'd live happily together in our shining sunset years.

I was naïve and utterly unrealistic.

I was also a little lonely at times, without the one-on-one close bond of a romantic relationship. I had lost my adored husband of 46 years in 2008, and after nine years of widowhood, there was no new wonderful companion on the horizon. My friends knew of no man who would be right for me. As for meeting someone in the supermarket, at a party, at a lecture, or some other "proper" place—well, that never happened.

I have always been a competent, independent, active, and successful woman, so I was doing very well on my own, but I missed the companionship, the giving and receiving of love. It was time to be proactive.

So, like millions of people of all ages and demographics, I signed up for two dating services. After two months, I realized why my friends hadn't "fixed me up," and despite the inventory of men, no one interested me. (This will make perfect sense if you've experienced online dating or know someone who has.)

Just as I was ready to cancel my useless memberships, a new, very pleasant face appeared. I was curious enough to check out his profile, which was very impressive. Then I read about his background, education, professional accomplishments, and interests, which were equally impressive.

There was just one little problem ... if you can call 3,000 miles *little*.

The glaring mis-match was that he lived in Atlanta, Georgia, and I lived in Newport Beach, California. I noticed that he had viewed my profile and photo, so with tongue in check, a cavalier attitude, and the perfunctory introductory words, I composed the following message:

> *"Thank you for checking out my profile. Obviously, I did the same with yours and find that we have numerous common interests. I know this sounds very shallow, but according to the site, we are a 100% match. However, there was a computer glitch. The one thing they neglected to factor in is that you're in Atlanta and I'm in Newport Beach. If your travels ever take you back to Southern California, please feel free to contact me."*

I never expected more than a polite acknowledgement and agreement. I had faith that he was a gentleman and would respond in kind. And he did ...

"Thanks, Susan. I will definitely contact you. I have very good friends who live in Newport Beach. I sometimes stay with them when I'm in town. When I was growing up, we had a summer house in Balboa near the point. I remember those times, as well as the evenings at the Fun Zone at the Pavilion."

That was July 7, 2017. Fast-forward two months, and we were planning to move in together, much to the surprise of my friends and chagrin of my family. No one was more surprised than I was, but I was also excited. As a senior looking for love in cyberspace, I was ready for a new beginning, and maybe even a happy ending.

Our relationship quickly developed, and Stephen and I appreciated the extraordinary story we were weaving, so much so that Stephen suggested we share it with others in the form of a book. Since we were both published authors, it was only natural that besides sharing our adventures, we'd also share a writing experience. I was intrigued about what he would say. How differently did a man see and interpret the same experiences, conversations, and emotional connection? So, we both started putting our thoughts, and then chapters, on paper, not knowing what the other was saying about our journey. What developed is this book, which includes not only our personal interpretations, but also snippets from the "love letters" (i.e., emails) that we shared during the beginning of our romance.

If there's one thing we hope you will take away from our story, it's that one is never too old to learn new lessons about life, love, and relationships. We both did.

Stephen
Atlanta, GA

AGE	HEIGHT	ETHNICITY
75	6'0"	White

 Message

 Send A Smile

More About Stephen . . .

Body Type	Athletic
Hair	Salt and Pepper
Religious Affiliation	Jewish
Political Views	Liberal
Occupation	Scientist, writer
Children	2 Adult
Level of Education	Ph.D.
Income	Self-sufficient
Smoke	No
Drink	Socially
Willing to Relocate	Yes
Interests	Art, travel, wine, cars

Susan

Corona del Mar, CA

AGE	HEIGHT	ETHNICITY
76	5'2"	White

 Message   Send A Smile

More About Susan . . .

Body Type	Slender
Hair	Red
Religious Affiliation	Jewish
Political Views	Conservative
Occupation	Author, speaker, entrepreneur
Children	2 Adult
Level of Education	Masters Degree +
Income	Self-sufficient
Smoke	No
Drink	Socially
Willing to Relocate	No
Interests	Theatre, travel, art, movies, yoga, walking

SECTION 1

. . . . .

*Before There
Was You*

A Good Girl Grows Up

~ Sue ~

Inever expected to find myself dating again, much less online. I thought I was done with that dance, because Larry and I would either live forever or die together peacefully in our sleep when we were well into our 90s. In fact, we were both always pretty healthy, so centennial birthdays didn't seem entirely out of the question. But alas, I ended up back in the dating pool, and these days, that dating pool seems to exist mostly online.

Growing up in a middle-class, Jewish family with high expectations, I was one of those very good girls who followed the subliminal path of the values held by my parents and extended family. The plan was to marry in a white gown, have children, raise them perfectly, and pass down those values to subsequent generations.

I can only imagine their reaction if they knew that I met a

total stranger through an online dating service and intended to spend the rest of my life with someone who could be a con artist or even a serial killer.

Suffice to say, that's just not how I was raised.

Of course, online dating wasn't a thing back then, but it would certainly have been frowned upon by my traditional family, especially for their prized daughter.

I was born on a Friday the 13th in Brooklyn, New York. War was raging in Europe, but my parents considered it a very lucky day for the Covell family. Their cute, redheaded baby girl came into the world with the promise of hope for better times. I joined my 3-year-old brother and completed our relatively comfortable family. Times were not easy, but as a baby and toddler, I was unaware of anything but love and having my needs met.

My early childhood memories are mostly positive, except for the inordinate number of deaths in my close-knit extended family. I learned about loss at a young age, while learning how to protect myself from painful emotions. I mastered that ability with ease and have carried it with me throughout my life.

Elementary and middle school were good times. My world expanded, and I had countless friends. I was a student leader, excelled academically, and was anxious to move on from my familiar life.

High school was a paradox for me. I loved it and found great satisfaction and confidence in my accomplishments, joining every club and society, participating in this sheltered mini world. The downside was that most of my family members were older, ill, suffering, and dying. The sound of an ambulance resonated with me. It often meant that someone I loved and counted on was on a stretcher being carted off to the hospital, or worse, the morgue.

I was needed at home and rushed through high school and college, completing them both a year early. I didn't have the luxury of going out of state for college; I was an integral part of the functioning and care of my family.

Despite my family and academic commitments, I dated a great deal. Having easy access to the exciting lights and glamour of Manhattan, my social life was full. I had many boyfriends, but none with serious intentions. However, there were two young men who were particularly special to me.

Craig and I spent a great deal of time together, but back then, it was common to have a date with someone on Friday night and someone else on Saturday night, unless you were going "steady." We weren't. Although our romance never took off with permanence, my friendship with Craig has stood the test of time. Today, over half a century later, we still have a connection, talk periodically, exchange holiday cards and even emails, and will always share a deep fondness.

Jimmy was also special to me. We enjoyed each other's company, had mutual friends, and were very happy together, but our goals were different. He was destined to start his career in the military, and I knew higher academia would be my path.

While I was busy dating, most of my friends were getting married, but there were still no strong prospects on my horizon. It never occurred to me to select one of these wonderful young men for my future. I was still young, not even 21 years old. Of course, in the '50s and '60s, getting married in your late teens or early 20s was the norm. The standard saying was that the only reason for a girl to go to college was to get her MRS degree. Today's generation would view this as insane and offensive, and perhaps it was. But that was a different time.

I wasn't too concerned about finding a husband. My mother always told me that it only took one ... and how right she was.

Everything changed when my relationship with one of the best-looking boys in our crowd took a turn. We went to a movie and dinner one Christmas Eve as friends, but by the time the evening was over, it seemed that some magic dust had been sprinkled over us, and we both knew, then and there, that this was more than friendship. Within six weeks, we were engaged.

I'd had a crush on Larry for years, but it took him until that night to realize that we were meant to be together "'til death do us part." And part us it did.

Portrait of the Dater as a Young Man

~ Stephen ~

I was born and raised in various parts of West Los Angeles. My parents liked to remodel houses, so we always seemed to be moving to a new neighborhood. They often went for Sunday drives and visited open houses. Upon returning home, they would tell me and my brother that they just made an offer. We moved so often that I attended five primary schools, one junior high, and two high schools. That's eight schools in 12 years. I found it difficult leaving childhood friends and changing schools, particularly in the middle of a school year. Perhaps that's why I was shy and stuttered.

My parents were both Jewish, but I didn't have a very Jewish upbringing. Both of my father's parents died when he was a young boy, and he became disillusioned with religion, so I never attended Sunday School or learned much about our faith. We observed some of the customs with other family members. For example, we celebrated Passover every year at my aunt and uncle's home. We also had a Christmas tree and celebrated the holiday with lots of presents. I remember going to bed early on Christmas Eve in anticipation of Santa's visit.

When I was approaching 13 years of age, my parents (mostly my father) decided I should have a bar mitzvah. Because I had never learned to read or speak Hebrew, they hired a tutor for me. I think it would have been easier teaching a rock to read Hebrew. This was also evident to the tutor, because as my bar mitzvah date approached, he had me memorize what I needed to say. I faked (and stuttered) my way through the service and made my parents proud.

Once I turned 16 and could drive, it became a bit easier to maintain friendships. I also started to date. My parents gave me curfews, which led to some mild resentment towards my brother, who was four years younger but never had a curfew. Perhaps I proved to them that they raised responsible children.

We didn't have texting back then, thus I had to make my dates using the telephone. Given my stutter, I was uncomfortable phoning for a date. One of the girl's parents would usually answer, and I always stammered trying to ask for their daughter. It was very embarrassing, but I fought through it and had dates on most Saturday nights.

Of course, I was always a perfect gentleman. I dated a girl named Gail during senior year of high school. We would go out and then back to her house, where we would sit on the living room couch reading the cartoon section from the Sunday paper. I was too clueless to realize that she was expecting me to kiss her, and never did. Later, she used me to make another boy jealous. I still think about that incident after all these years, but that's another story.

I still had a lot to learn about women, but I was a decent student. In high school, I hardly ever studied, as I relied on a very good memory to get through my classes. I really didn't think much about college. I never visited schools or consulted with my guidance counselor. My default plan was to attend Santa Monica City College for two years and then transfer to a four-year college.

During my first semester at Santa Monica City College, I was trying to impress a woman I met in class, so I signed up to run for Men's Student Body Treasurer. As it happened, I was the only candidate for this obscure office. In a quirk of fate, I became Men's Student Body President when both the newly elected president and vice president failed to make their grades. The next semester I ran for Men's Student Body President on my own and then Commissioner of Finance. I won both elections.

I felt that I was on my way. To what, remained to be determined. I still stuttered, which affected my ability and desire to speak in public. But I pushed myself out of my comfort zone, and the better I got at public speaking, the less I stuttered.

There were two events that I believe were particularly important in helping me overcome my affliction. The first was at my school's annual Sports Awards Banquet. As Men's Student Body President, I had to MC the event. The speaker that year was Rafer Johnson, who had won the gold medal in the decathlon at the 1960 Olympics. I sat next to him during dinner, and as the time to introduce him approached, I became visibly nervous. I remember him talking to me to calm me down and telling me that I just needed to relax and everything would be OK. I was really impressed that he would take the time to offer me advice, and I kept his words in mind as I took the stage. The second event occurred several years later, during graduate school. I was taking a class that I really liked but never asked questions for fear of stuttering. During one of the last classes, I really wanted to ask a question, so I took a deep breath, told myself that I wasn't going to stutter, and asked my question. I haven't stuttered (much) since that day.

After my sophomore year of undergrad, I transferred to San Jose State University. Living away from home enabled me to concentrate more on my studies, and my grades quickly improved, but I still maintained an active social life. I joined a fraternity and dated often.

Then, at the end of my junior year, I met my first true love, Shirley. I was infatuated with her. I saw her during the summer when she and her mother visited San Jose, and later she visited me in Los Angeles. We became "pinned" that fall.

I applied to several medical schools, hoping to eventually follow my dream (and my parents' dream) of becoming a physician. When I graduated in January 1964, I was still waiting to hear if I would be accepted. However, medical school classes didn't begin until September. Many of my friends were getting their military obligation out of the way, and the draft board told me that I might be drafted if I didn't remain in school. So, I moved home and began taking a few graduate-level classes at San Fernando Valley State College. To make some spending money, I also worked as a teaching assistant for one of my professors, Dr. Robert Mah.

Then came a day that I will never forget. It was April 6, 1964. My father hadn't been feeling well for some time and needed exploratory surgery. Afterwards, I visited him in the hospital, where he told me and my brother that he had pancreatic cancer. At the time, there were few treatments for this form of cancer (there are still few options). I felt frustrated that more couldn't be done. Thankfully, my father seemed to recuperate well from the surgery. He went back to work and even took some trips with my mother. For the next few months, I didn't notice any effect of the cancer on my father. However, the fact that medical science could do little for my father made me decide to forgo becoming a physician and go into research instead.

That summer, Dr. Mah informed me that he was leaving San Fernando Valley State College to accept a faculty position at the School of Public Health at the University of North Carolina (UNC) in Chapel Hill, North Carolina. He said I showed promise and asked me to go with him as his Ph.D. graduate student in the field of microbiology. The offer came with a full scholarship that would cover my tuition and living expenses.

I didn't want to be so far from my father while he was sick, but he encouraged me to take this opportunity if it was something I really wanted to do. I also asked Shirley for her opinion. We had been drifting apart, but still I was half hoping she would ask me to stay in California and go to medical school. Her response—"I don't care"—sealed the deal.

I was a liberal, Jewish Californian heading to the South during the tumultuous '60s. I didn't know what to expect and felt both excited and terrified about my decision. I left Los Angeles for Chapel Hill in late August on my first transcontinental flight. I changed planes in Atlanta, where I met my cousin Greg for the first time at the airport. He was an undergraduate student at UNC and promised to keep in touch with me while I was there.

Dr. Mah met me at the Raleigh-Durham airport. At the age of 22, my graduate education had begun, but was almost derailed when my father passed away that October. I flew home for the funeral and drove back to Chapel Hill, which gave me plenty of time to think about how much I would miss my father and how much I wanted his approval. I decided I would honor him by working hard and being successful in my career.

Most of my grad school classmates were older and had returned to school after working for several years. I knew no one (except my cousin Greg), so I initially moved into my fraternity house at UNC. Being with "brothers" helped me ease into the situation, but the party atmosphere made it difficult to concentrate on my studies, so I moved into a rented house with Daniel Vicenti, a fellow graduate student who was a full-blooded Navajo Indian from Gallup, New Mexico. He was very outspoken and opened my eyes about what it was like being an American Indian and growing up on a reservation. For Halloween, he dressed as a member of the Ku Klux Klan and walked down the main street of Chapel Hill, hood and all. Not a smart thing to do in the South, but he made it through unscathed.

Not long after, Greg fixed me up with a woman from Monroe, North Carolina, a small town north of Charlotte. She invited me to her home for lunch to meet her parents, who questioned me about my upbringing. I remembered the sage advice my parents had given me when I left Los Angeles—"There are two things you shouldn't talk about: religion and politics." Thankfully, I avoided those taboo subjects. After lunch, her father and brother excused themselves from the table, went to the closet, got their robes and hoods, and headed to a KKK rally. That was the last time I saw her.

Soon I started dating Kathy, a fellow graduate student. She was very attractive, and I was smitten, but she was not interested in a meaningful relationship, so we kept things light. She often talked about her friend, Ruth, who would be attending our school that fall.

A couple years later, Ruth became my first wife.

From Blushing Bride
to Weeping Widow

~ Sue ~

At age 20, I fell in love for the first (and I believed, last) time. The marriage and intensity of feelings were going to last forever and never be marred by real life, I just knew it.

Larry and I married in 1962, moved away from our world in 1966, and never looked back. Our ties to Brooklyn (and our past) had already diminished. In the first few years of our marriage, I lost both my parents, my grandmother, four aunts and uncles, friends of parents, and extended family. Larry lost his dad.

So, we dusted ourselves off, discarded our funeral outfits, and began to build a loving and successful life together in sunny California.

I had graduated *cum laude* from college, early, with a master's degree in education and psychology, so it wasn't hard to find work. Before I married, my first official teaching position was working with intellectually gifted fifth and sixth graders in a silk-stocking area of Brooklyn. When we moved to California, I effortlessly found a teaching position in another silk-stocking neighborhood in Marin County

Soon after, we had our first child. I felt it was important to be at home with her, and our second daughter during their formative years, and that's what I did.

I loved being their mother and giving them all the love and positive direction I could. However, once they were both in school, I knew it was time to go back to work—not because we needed the money, but because I needed something more in my life. Overachiever that I had always been, I embarrassingly admit I wasn't content as a housewife. Granted, being a working mother was not a popular choice in those decades, and it was challenging, but I did my best to do a good job at both.

That's when I began my journey as a serial entrepreneur. I loved the challenge of starting businesses, bringing them to success, and then moving onto another new challenge. Among my endeavors were: Olympiad Tutoring Agency; The Left-Handed Complement, a self-explanatory catalog company; ExecuGift corporate buying services; Motivation Resources, a full-service incentive corporation; and my favorite, International Travel Incentives, which I owned and loved for close to 30 years.

Along with my entrepreneurial endeavors, I was also PR director of an international firm and an assistant therapist for Transactional Analysis. I stayed busy, traveled often, and still made time for my daughters ... and for Larry.

We were both entrepreneurs, worked hard, played hard, traveled the world, and loved our family more than anything. In 46 years of marriage, we had the expected ups and downs, but we cherished the luxurious life we had created, and most importantly, our lasting bond. Most of those years were wonderful. I felt love, comfort, protection, and promise with him.

Then, the unthinkable happened. My seemingly invincible husband was diagnosed with acute myeloid leukemia and passed away after 10 agonizing months.

For the next three years, both my life and career were at a standstill. I closed the business I loved. I was too deep in my grief to think about work ... much less romance.

The desire to work came back first. After years of feeling lost and disconnected, my business juices finally started to flow again. At first, it was just a slow trickle, but in 2011, I discovered what I wanted to do. I would put everything I had learned in the years since Larry's passing to good use, and help other people avoid some of the grief and overwhelming emotions that I went through.

With the encouragement of a dear friend, I created a methodology for handling the logistics of loss. I began a consulting firm called Chaos to Control, and wrote my first book, *Driving Solo: Dealing with Grief and the Business of Financial Survival.* I spent several years talking about the business of grief on the speaking circuit and promoting my book on radio and television and in print media. When that initial flurry was over, I realized I still had more to say and more people to help. That's when I wrote *Later Is Too Late: Hard Conversations That Can't Wait.*

While I was enjoying my new career, I still wasn't ready for a new love. When Larry died, the years disappeared with him, but my love for him lived on in my mind and heart. It never died. I convinced myself that I'd already had my once-in-a-lifetime experience of love. It could, and probably would, never happen again.

But secretly, I wished that it would. I wanted to be half of that elderly couple walking arm in arm—the couple I saw in senior magazines and ads for the latest medications promising vitality and longevity. The couple Larry and I had fantasized about being.

Only, where was I supposed to find the other half? I had maintained my female and couple friends, but as a single woman, now 70 years old, the future looked anything but exciting. I was feeling down.

Even my doctor knew it.

"You've got to get out more, Sue," he told me one day at his office. "Just have lunch or go online and meet a man, whatever it takes for you to start being your old vivacious, happy self."

He wasn't the first person to tell me this, not by a long shot. But the words seemed to make more sense coming from my doctor. He was younger than I, but he had been in our lives for many years. When Larry became ill, he was there; when Larry died, he was a pallbearer and even asked for one of his golf clubs as a remembrance. We were all close. I knew he cared about my well-being and I trusted him.

So, I followed his advice and went online that very evening in my new mission to start my female-male life again. My friends and I still laugh at the extreme caution I took with those first dates. I would let them know the name and telephone number of my date, where we were meeting, and what time they should expect to hear from me after our lunch rendezvous, which was always in a populated restaurant. If I didn't call them, they were instructed to dial 911 and report that I had been abducted by a criminal.

This was seven years ago, and I really pride myself for being wary at that point. I got my feet wet in the scene and gained a lot of confidence in the process.

I was very fortunate. After not too many such dates, I met a wonderful man with whom I had a seven-year, on-again, off-again, on-again, off-again, *ad infinitum* relationship. To this day, Bob and I are best friends, but our love story never fully developed. When we first met, I thought I was ready to begin a fresh chapter in my life. I was past the worst of my grief, and Bob was coming out of his second divorce. We were both excited for a fresh start.

I stopped online dating, feeling so happy. I felt that I had open eyes and saw all the good in my new relationship, as well as the obstacles we would need to overcome to make our romance work. Our personalities were very different. He was older and more settled. He had simplified his life and was less adventurous, more realistic, and less curious. But he was extremely bright, well-educated, handsome, and cultured. He lived generously, was loving and kind, and was very good to me.

We tried very hard to make it work, but in reality, he was ready for a more serious, committed relationship, and I was not. I denied it at the time, but I was still tightly clutching to the 46 years I had shared with Larry, my first intense and forever love.

The fascinating part of being with Bob was that every time we broke up, and it was often, we felt the need to be together and rekindled our feelings and relationship. It didn't work for us to be apart, but it also didn't work for us to be together. It simply wasn't meant to be.

As much as I wanted to be part of a couple, that's how much I wanted my freedom. I wanted no commitments, no routines. This was a new feeling for me, and the longer I lived alone, the more that way of life became ingrained in me. It was odd, since I had never felt tied down with Larry. We both had exciting separate business lives that we loved, which involved a great deal of travel, most often with our individual business associates. But Larry loved my business so much that he frequently traveled with me as well. My clients all adored him. He was a man's man and a lady's man. Some people assumed he was the corporate owner and I, the assistant. Those in the know always found it humorous that even in the 21st century, there was still that Old Boy's Club mentality.

Perhaps that was one of the reasons I found it hard to be with anyone else. I was still blinded by my youthful love and had Larry on a pedestal. In my eyes, he was the ideal man, and although I knew that it was foolish to compare Bob, or anyone else, to Larry, I was doing just that. I might not have admitted it at the time, but I was looking for a clone of Larry and I wasn't ready to expand my locked-in feelings.

I wondered, even then, if I would ever be able to let go of Larry and move on with someone else. But I wasn't giving up just yet.

A respectable, but rather short, three months after breaking off my romantic relationship with Bob, I decided to give dating another try and see if there was a companion out there waiting to meet me. So, I ventured online again with an open mind and a positive attitude—about my future in general, and about the idea of online dating.

If my relationship with Bob had taught me anything, it was that all the good ones *weren't* taken (or dead), and that perhaps there *was* something to this online dating thing.

❧

Life, Love, and Leading Ladies

~ Stephen ~

*U*nlike Sue, I didn't have one epic love story with a tragic ending. I had several shorter stories, each with a pretty common ending: divorce.

I got married for the first time at age 25, during my third year of grad school. The reason was pretty simple: I grew up in a society that equated being intimate with marriage. My wife-to-be was the first person I was intimate with, and so we got married.

Granted, she helped nudge things along. The summer before we got married, we drove to Los Angeles, where she met my mother. During the trip west, we talked about marriage, but we didn't make any firm plans. After returning to Chapel

Hill, she called my mother to thank her for hosting us and told her we were getting married. My mother was upset that I never mentioned it to her, and I felt that I was trapped into going through with the wedding.

In retrospect, this wasn't a strong foundation on which to build a lasting marriage.

When I completed my Ph.D., we moved to Athens, Georgia, where I spent a year as a postdoctoral fellow, and where our daughter was born. I then accepted a faculty position at Southeastern Massachusetts University and moved us to North Dartmouth.

My wife and I argued a lot, and she would often go home to her parents, who lived a few miles away. It was not a good situation, so after four and a half years together, we decided to end our marriage.

After a year at Southeastern Massachusetts University, I accepted a position at the Harvard School of Public Health. For the next three years, I had a wonderful time being both single in Boston and a faculty member at Harvard. Then in 1974, I met my future second wife.

We hit it off quickly, but our timing was bad. I had just accepted a faculty position at Oregon Health Sciences University in Portland. Rather than going our separate ways, we decided to get married and move west together. In retrospect, we should have waited. The relationship was rushed, and we didn't know each other as well as we should have. Nevertheless, we moved to Portland and got married that summer. Our son was born in 1977.

From the beginning, our relationship was troubled. Rhona was resentful and jealous of my ex-wife and daughter, and she did not want me to be part of my daughter's life. We got divorced in 1981 after about seven years.

I was single once again and dated several women during this period, including a woman who helped me re-establish a relationship with my daughter. I will always be thankful for that.

In 1984, I accepted a position at the Centers for Disease Control (CDC) in Atlanta, which unfortunately meant moving away from my son. It also meant starting a new life in an unfamiliar city where I knew very few people. The silver lining was that my daughter would be living with me.

In December 1985, I met a woman who would become my third wife. This time, I refused to rush into things. We dated for more than two and a half years before getting married in 1988. I thought this marriage would last for the rest of my life.

I worked at the CDC for more than 30 years and retired in November 2014. A short while later, I found myself single again after 28 years of marriage. It was an amicable split, and I had sufficient finances to start my life over again. However, I returned to work part-time to ease the financial strain of buying, remodeling, and furnishing my new house, where I lived all alone.

Nearly three decades had passed since I was actively dating. This was a new era, and I was somewhat out of date on how to meet women, so I approached my newfound singleness with some trepidation. My contact with eligible women was mostly centered around work, and I was not interested in the potential drama associated with dating a co-worker. I am a social drinker (mostly wine) but did not feel comfortable frequenting bars to meet women. I am also somewhat reserved and felt awkward about chatting up strangers. It seemed my only options were being fixed up by friends or computer dating.

I had hired a decorator shortly after I bought my home. Several months into my project, she asked if I would be interested in meeting a friend of hers who had been widowed for about two years. I gave the friend a call, and we began dating. She was born in the U.S. but had been raised in France and Venezuela. I was the first person she had dated in about 30 years, so we had something in common. We went out a couple of times a week for about four or five months.

During this time, I enjoyed her companionship, plus it enabled me to transition, albeit slowly, to single life in the 21st century. I was able to learn what I wanted and what I didn't want in a relationship.

It was also during this time that I decided to try computer dating.

Single and Senior—
What's Next?

~ Sue ~

When I shared with my good friends that I was dating online again, most of them thought it was a great idea, filled with an attitude of youthfulness and possibilities.

But often it's the naysayers who leave an impression. From them, I heard ...

"What's the point of starting over in your golden years? How can you be lonely when you have children and grandchildren nearby, and a close circle of great friends? Do you really want to fall in love again, only to have him die, or become sick and need you to be his caregiver? What's so bad about being single at your age?"

These are the kinds of questions people tend to ask (or want to ask) seniors looking for love. I understand where they're coming from, and I understand the risks, but I'm here to tell you those risks can be worth it.

It's a couple's world, and we all know it. When you have a partner, there's an ease to daily life and decisions. If you want to go to dinner, see a movie, travel, visit family, or do a myriad of other activities, you consult with your partner and decide whether to go. As a single person, when you're inclined to do any of the aforementioned activities, or bounce an idea off someone, or even just feel the presence of another body, it becomes a series of complicated steps.

First, you must think of who might be available. Anyone who's married is probably too busy with their partner, so you don't bother to call them. Next, you start dialing until you find someone whose schedule aligns with yours. Of course, spontaneity doesn't enter this scenario. So, you pull out your calendar and see what day, week, or month you can coordinate time and interest.

Sometimes it's just plain not worth the effort. I've learned to forge ahead, but it takes a lot of self-talking and grit.

On a practical level, it simply isn't convenient to be alone. It takes work to create your life. It's hard when you must make major decisions solo. There are always financial, governmental, family, and maintenance issues to deal with, and other problems that pop up when you least expect them. I often wonder if trouble secretly waits until you're stressed with one issue, so the other problems can join in to give you that triple whammy.

Who can relieve you of some of this burden? Of course, you

can always reach out to someone, but if it's not your partner, it's often an imposition, or at least it feels like one. And no one wants to feel they are intruding on someone else's busy life.

Social situations are also inconvenient and often uncomfortable. Look around at restaurants, parties, and other events. You see mostly couples. How often do you see a third or fifth wheel at that lovely candlelit restaurant, the fun party, the movie, etc.? And when you receive invitations to events, they say "and guest." Who is this mystery person who is supposed to accompany you to the event?

If you're brave, and I am, you'll go to many places by yourself. I usually have a good time, but as independent as I am, I can't help but notice that I'm one of the few single people there. Is everybody else hiding, or do they just choose not to attend rather than be the odd man out?

Part of the problem is that couples tend to go out with other couples. If you're newly divorced or widowed, you'll most likely be included at first. But before long, the couples go back to their original pattern—being with other couples. I completely understand this and hold no resentment. It's just the way things work ... and the older you get, the harder it gets.

So, what do you do when you've reached an age where these daily and special events seem too much to do alone? Where do you turn when you realize that you want companionship— maybe not on a 24/7 basis, but you want to share the highs and lows of your life with a partner?

You could ask your friends to set you up, attend church functions, take up a sport, go to a class, or do some other acceptable group activity in hopes of meeting someone. When you've exhausted all these outlets, what's left in the 21st century? Online dating.

Of course, online dating isn't a guarantee. It's challenging at any age, but when you're a senior (especially a woman senior), the playing field is narrower. The most noticeable reason for the dwindling of potential men is that, sadly, they die before women, and widowers don't stay single long. The rich ones often get swept up by younger women. Then there are stories of the "Brisket Brigade." As soon as a man loses his wife, friendly neighbors, distant friends, and single friends of friends show up on his doorstep to nourish the lonely man. The way to his heart is through his stomach, and suddenly he's inundated with brisket, lasagna, and chicken casseroles from well-meaning women with ulterior motives. It often works. Statistics show that most widowers are married or in a serious relationship within a year after losing their wives.

Moral of the story for single senior women: One must be ready to pounce. You might be out of luck if you wait too long.

In all seriousness, cooking for grieving men isn't exactly my style of wooing, though I certainly don't judge those women for their methods. And as I decided to take another plunge into online dating, I hoped that no one would judge me for mine.

Misadventures in Computer Dating

~ Stephen ~

Sue was not the first woman I met online. In fact, I had been online dating for a couple of months before we first crossed virtual paths. Some of the women I met online were quite nice, but I also had more than a few bad experiences.

Why put myself through that? Why would a man in his 70s want to date again? Why would a man who's been married three times want to marry again? The short answer is that I wanted to fall in love one last time and spend my remaining years with my best friend and lover.

The longer answer is that I was accustomed to being in a relationship and sharing my life with someone I loved. I missed that.

I've never minded spending time alone, and I had many things to keep me occupied, but most of them involved just me, and I wanted to share some of these activities with a loved one. I was always happier and healthier with a partner. As a single man, I stayed up later than I normally would. Perhaps it was the sound of the television I left on for company. Or perhaps it was the political nightmare we were living through (and still are). I've worked in nine administrations, both Republican and Democrat, and have never seen the rancor and partisanship that exists today. That alone was enough to keep me up worrying about the future of our country and what the future would be like for my granddaughter.

I needed someone with whom I could discuss current events and who could keep me grounded. Also, cooking for one can be detrimental to my weight, as well as a bit lonely. My children and granddaughter do not live nearby, so I don't see them very often. I have friends but rarely hang out with the guys. In fact, most of my friends are women (some married, some single). But having friends isn't the same thing as having a partner.

I had seen a couple of commercials on television touting particular dating sites, so I started with one of those. I filled out my profile, added a couple of recent pictures (of me and my dog), and paid the membership fee. I thought the responses would come rolling in. And at first, they did, but most were from women who were at least 30 years younger than me and resided out of state. After a private message or two, many of them wanted to get off the site and communicate by phone, text, or personal email accounts.

I should have read the small print (and warnings) about scams, because suddenly I was being deluged by women with unbelievable sob stories. One woman had traveled from Chattanooga, Tennessee, to London to buy antiques but ran out of money and couldn't get home to her daughter. Another was an artist from Indiana who had gone to the Philippines for an art show and couldn't pay the duty on her paintings. She had trouble getting back to the U.S., and when she was finally on the way to the airport, she was in an automobile accident and wound up in a local hospital where, according to an email from her lawyer, she had died from her extensive injuries. But first she had made *me* the beneficiary of her inheritance (why, I'll never know), which was in a bank in South Africa. I simply needed to pay bank fees and taxes in order to claim it.

Another woman from San Antonio purportedly had a jewelry company that made gold chains for larger stores. She said that she had won a contract from a Pennsylvania company to manufacture the chains (she even sent me a picture of the contract) but had to travel to the Philippines to purchase the metal. She took her son with her, and once there, she didn't have enough money to pay the tax, her hotel bill, or her return plane fare.

Then there was the army nurse deployed to Afghanistan who didn't have money for food. She also was soliciting donations for Afghan orphans, but the address she gave me to send the money was in Accra, Ghana. Apparently, Ghana is a popular place for scammers, as several women claimed to be visiting relatives who lived in Ghana but didn't have the money to return to the U.S.

Finally, there was the Polish woman from Las Vegas who wanted me to help her get her $7 million inheritance. All I had to do was pay the tax and fees, and she would give me 10 percent, plus interest.

Many of these stories defied logic and required me to suspend my disbelief; however, they still resonated with a lonely man. I quickly learned just how many people prey on unsuspecting singles looking for relationships on these dating sites. You can never even be completely sure if you're communicating with a woman or man, or where they are located. Many of the pictures that people post look fake. Some of the sites do a better job than others in removing these fake profiles. For example, on one site, I saw several profiles that had a phone number written on the picture or embedded within the profile. Many of these were deleted by the site within 24 hours; however, I wonder how many desperate men called those numbers before they were removed.

Thankfully, I was not desperate enough to fall for any of the scams. Nor was I deterred. I knew I was not the only single senior who was legitimately looking for love. If I just gave it some time, perhaps the right woman would come along.

Online Dating: Take 2

~ Sue ~

In the Spring of 2017, I signed up for two dating services. I had been warned that filling out my profile would be an arduous task. On the contrary, I found it easy because I was completely open and honest. There was no point embellishing anything since it would only come back to bite me on the first date. It helped that I had experience writing about myself. I'd already written two books, both of which shared my life story, and I had helped friends write their stories.

I quickly checked off the mandatory boxes—gender, age, location, sexual orientation, etc.—but I took a little longer on the essay "selling" myself. I decided to be concise, hit the highlights, and keep it light.

Choosing my profile pic was a little tougher. Again, my

mantra was truthfulness, so I narrowed it down to current photos. Still, I understood why some people use less-than-recent images. We tend to see ourselves as we did in our best years, except when catching a glimpse of ourselves in a mirror, or worse yet, seeing a photo. In my mind, I'm still young, but on camera, I'm not. What happened to that cheerleader?

Of course, the same is true of *men* in my age group. They all look so very old ... way too old for me. This is a dilemma I seem to share with all my female friends. We're often more attracted to men who are 10 or 20 years younger than we are. Of course, it's absurd, but when we feel so young and vibrant, we insanely think it makes sense. Still, back to the older men we go.

Older though I am, I still look good for my age, and when I first joined online dating sites, I also had new-girl-on-the-block status. I received a huge amount of interest, or more accurately, curiosity. It was flattering and ego-enhancing, but very unrealistic. What were these men thinking? We had zero in common, and there was no foundation on which to try to build a relationship. Were they fishing, looking for a good time, trying to fill up space? Whatever it was, I excluded them from my possibilities.

None of my matches came close to my idea of an ideal mate. We all have our wish lists and our (more realistic) must-have lists. Of the utmost importance to me were education, career, zest for life, appropriate age range, high activity level, serious travel, interest in theatre, financial security, and family orientation.

It's a long list, I know, but I have high standards. And although I was lonely at times, I was not desperate enough to be very compromising.

I politely responded to the matches who didn't seem to meet enough of my needs. I still had traditional manners and hadn't taken on the new "ghosting" protocol. The few dates I accepted were very pleasant lunches, but none led to a second date. Cross off those who only talked about themselves, didn't have gentlemanly manners, were too anxious, or were looking for a financial partner. Pretty soon, there was no one left.

After a few months of this, I decided I was done. Just as I was preparing to cancel my subscriptions, I received what claimed to be a 100-percent match. *Hmm,* I thought as I clicked on the message. *Maybe I'm not done after all.*

It was certainly worth the few minutes it took to read Stephen's profile and look at the photo. He was tall, which was good. I've always gravitated towards men over 6', even though I'm only 5'2". He had strong, commanding features, looked like he took good physical care of himself, and was serious. There was no toothy smile, and he was dressed in a suit and tie. It was a professional headshot, but then again, my main photo was the same.

Sure enough, this man was a possibility—the first one that piqued my interest.

His bio was even more promising. He was extremely accomplished in his field, held many degrees and awards, was still actively working and writing, and sounded interested in life. He had been to more than 90 countries, so he shared my passion for travel. (Not that I'm keeping score, but I had traversed more than 120.) He also shared my interest in theatre, dining, family, and wine. We had similar religious backgrounds and were close in age. He even grew up in California, where I lived, and he visited frequently.

What I found most appealing about his profile was that he was highly educated and accomplished, obviously a type-A overachiever. Just like me.

At age 76, I still felt compelled to create, to write, and to participate in the professional world. And if I was going be someone's life partner, I wanted someone who still felt young, useful, and relevant.

Clearly, Stephen did.

I took the next step. I sent my cavalier message about his profile and the computer glitch that paired us up, despite the fact we lived 3,000 miles apart, and offered to meet him if he was ever in my area. To me, that was the end of that. To him, it wasn't.

✉ Inbox Insights

July 16

Sue: *"I don't want to belabor a point, and if I'm out of line, please tell me so. I carefully read about your out-of-state experiences, and it sounds like you've met high-quality people. What do you plan to do about the geographical complications? Are you looking for interesting conversation or how do you see following through? I'm finding that dating men who are 60-70 miles away is challenging."*

July 17

Stephen: *"I find your comments about long-distance relationships appropriate. To be honest, I haven't thought it through in its entirety. Here are my current thoughts. If I only date women who are within 50 miles, I may miss meeting the right person. So, the question becomes, how do I deal with the geographical complications of such a relationship? I was thinking that at our age, we have more free time to travel and meet initially. If there is 'something' there, then we could plan to spend more time together (vacations, trips, etc.). In the meantime, we could write, talk, and Skype to get to know one another better. Also, with today's traffic, a 3.5-hour flight might take less time than a 70-mile drive. This isn't like the 1940s, when a train trip across the U.S. took three to four days."*

SECTION 2

. . . . .

*The Beginning of a
Beautiful Romance*

76 Going on 16

~ Sue ~

Do you remember your first crush, your first love that changed every part of you? You were no longer just living; you were suddenly thrust into a state of emotional, intellectual, physical, and perhaps non-rational being. Ask a teenager or a millennial if you could replicate this feeling as a senior, and I'm certain they'd roll their eyes. I'm here to differ with them.

I've only experienced the floating-on-air kind of love twice—once as a giddy 20-year-old and once as a giddy 76-year-old.

When I first started corresponding with Stephen, I found myself anticipating every email with excitement. Soon, warmth and comfort crept into our conversations. Gradually, as the relationship began to evolve, my emotions began to heighten.

Without even having met this man, I noticed my pulse racing when I thought about him. Sometimes my heart even pounded. I didn't fall asleep without him on my mind. I fantasized about being together. I was simply happy.

Not only was I excited about him. I felt comfortable opening up to him and sharing my honest opinions. Like Stephen (and most people, really), I've been taught not to discuss socially taboo topics like politics, religion, and money until I feel safe in an environment or relationship. I think when meeting a stranger through online dating, it's wise to be ultra-cautious before opening up a can of worms that could turn ugly, so I tread gently in my early email correspondence with Stephen. But as the days turned into weeks of communicating, these subjects gradually entered our conversations.

Details weren't necessary regarding money. From our past adventures and present way of life, we both seemed to be financially secure and weren't too out of sync. We later discovered that East Coast living and West Coast living were economically far apart, but we could work that out.

We met on a Jewish dating site, so religion took care of itself. Our families handled traditions differently, but having the common archetype ingrained for generations, we both *felt* Jewish. Although that was not a major criterion in finding a partner, it certainly made things less complicated. It provided common ground, as we understood each other's attitudes, histories, expressions, stories, food references, and even jokes.

Test one passed. A-plus.

Then came politics. Stephen quickly broached that subject

by telling me that he was liberal in thought and actions and had strong and open opinions. I wasn't very vocal at first and said just enough to be politically correct and avoid confrontation. But I did assure him that I shared some of his concerns about the current administration, as did many people. That seemed to make him feel better.

That said, Stephen and I weren't in lock-step politically. I know that many people from other parts of the country think everyone in California is liberal, but I am a registered Republican and conservative. When I was a child, both my parents worked for and supported the Republican Party, which was quite an anomaly in a predominately ultra-liberal, Jewish community in Brooklyn. I'm also a free-thinker and try to be open-minded and not vote along party lines. There are aspects of the party's beliefs with which I disagree, but I am fiscally conservative, having been a business owner most of my adult life. Larry and I agreed in this area, although I was more tempered.

Despite our differences, Stephen and I were able to listen to each other's viewpoints, even though I found Stephen to be at the far end of the spectrum compared to me. We never tried to convince each other of our leanings but had very civil discussions, and often found ourselves in agreement on a particular issue. He had his preferred news station, and I was happy to listen to his favorite commentators, not necessarily agreeing or disagreeing.

Test two? Maybe a B-minus. Still a passing grade.

Having broached these topics and cleared the potential hurdles, we knew that our feelings for each other would be stronger than those taboo topics, and we were free to delve deeper into the relationship.

Even after we'd been writing to each other for several weeks, Stephen never suggested we have a phone conversation. In retrospect, I can see how easy it is to fall in love with the written word—whether it's in a romantic way like the story of Cyrano de Bergerac, or in an inexplicable way, like the tales of women falling in love with serial killers behind bars, all through letters. Either way, when we write, we have the opportunity to carefully choose our words and delete what doesn't feel comfortable. We can be creative and clever, and we don't have to respond to the other person in the moment. We can, in turn, re-read what we receive and use our imaginations to fill in the blanks.

Our relationship went on this way for almost two months. Friends would ask me how often we spoke, and I was somewhat embarrassed to say that we had not spoken at all yet. Not only were they surprised; it had me questioning the situation. So, I made the next move (not in character for me, but I had nothing to lose) and suggested we use the telephone to talk. Stephen agreed, but with our mutually busy schedules and the time difference, spontaneity was not an option, so we arranged a time that would work for both of us.

೩❀೨

✉ INBOX INSIGHTS

July 29

Stephen: *"I feel like a teenager thinking about speaking to you on the phone. I am looking forward to an in-person meeting. I know my stomach will feel all squishy before we meet. I don't know what will happen, but I'll go with the flow, so to speak."*

Aug 1

Sue: *"I agree it's time for us to speak on the phone, but it does add another dimension. The computer is so easy. There are no pauses, no second guessing. I was also thinking about what will happen when we meet. Let's agree in advance that there won't be any awkwardness. I don't know what that looks like, but it sounds good. It's nice to know we share that anxious teenage feeling."*

I made certain to be near the telephone at the appointed hour. I was filled with anticipation, excitement, and curiosity when I answered the phone. I already felt like I knew him so well, but this was a new level of intimacy.

I'll admit that first conversation was a little awkward. I remember thinking that his voice didn't match what I expected. What did I expect? I didn't know, but it wasn't what I heard. Without visual cues or experience talking to each other, we both had trouble determining when the other was finished talking, so we kept accidentally interrupting each other. Native American tribes have an expression for this: stepping on one's words.

That was the second problem I had. When I responded, since there were no visual clues, I thought the timing was appropriate, but in fact, I was stepping on his words. There were pregnant pauses, and our goodbyes were uncomfortable. Needless to say, this was hard for me. I'm extroverted, and I talk freely and lightly. Stephen is a lifelong scientist and an introvert, so he thinks and deliberates before responding. It took about a half-dozen calls before we communicated with ease.

Stephen eventually suggested that we make it a point to talk every other day, and I agreed. It was practical, and I viewed it as something someone with an organized mind would propose. The upside was that the emails continued daily. They were long and filled with news, questions, and ideas. More importantly, that's where we both put our most warm and revealing words.

The other positive aspect of this sporadic phone communication was that it made me aware of how much I missed him, his voice, and the closeness that our chats brought to the relationship. On days that Stephen was to call, I structured my entire schedule around that phone date.

Based on our long email exchanges, we already knew about each other's family, childhood, interests, work background, values, expectations, and beliefs. The territory of conversation then ran the gamut from the mundane of daily living, to places we had both explored, to the broader political situation of the country and world.

We also talked a lot about our relationship—the deeper personal concerns, what we wanted in a partnership, the roles our work schedules played in forming relationships. As time progressed, there were subtle innuendos about how we both had grown to feel very comfortable and close. Most importantly, we both valued honesty and openness, which has been my mantra throughout my life and seemed paramount to Stephen as well.

Having heard horror stories of people who had fallen for someone less than honest online, I suppose we were both naïve and trusting. I don't know why, but I never doubted his sincerity and truthfulness, and I, in turn, never expressed anything that was not real.

Still, as much as I believed that I could trust Stephen, I admit that I wanted verification. After all, whether you're 20 or 80, you've been warned about the dangers involved in pursuing online dating. Of course, everyone thinks they're too savvy to fall for any of this, but sometimes the other person has more street smarts and is oh so charming.

Each age group has its own caveats, but there are universal ones as well. I've learned through the informal Seniors Single

Society that women lie about their age and men about their height. The scammers are the elites, the downright liars are frightening, and the stretchers of truth bring disappointment. How about the photos that are 10 years old? Gravity can do a lot of damage in that time. What about the people who have others write their erudite and profound profiles? The list goes on and on.

We seniors are a particularly vulnerable group. We know that we've lived the greatest part of our lives and want to grab onto happiness, companionship, and love for our remaining time. We often wear blinders, ignore red flags, let our emotions take over, and make decisions that we would be appalled to discover our friends had made. I am guilty of being part of that club and am embarrassed in retrospect, but also proud of some of the actions I took.

It was easy for me to vet Stephen. I immediately Googled him (as I do every potential date) and learned that he had worked for the CDC for 28 years. I considered that a plus. He obviously had to undergo extreme scrutiny to get security clearance. I also discovered that we had mutual friends in California, and he had even given a lecture for a local community group. In an odd coincidence, I discovered that one of my closest friends, Patsy, went to high school with Stephen's cousin, Jerry, and they were still in contact.

Our mutual connections made me feel safer, and at the very least, I knew Stephen was real. He sent me photos of his home, inside and out, as well as his car. Of course, it could have been anybody's home and car, but at that point, I had a good feeling.

If I'd had any doubt, I would have had a background check

done, and it would have been worth the expense. I had too much to lose, emotionally and financially, and I'd been told that widows are very desirable, thanks to inherited wealth and insurance policies.

I didn't want to be one of those tragic stories. I wanted a love story, and the more I got to know Stephen, the more I believed he would be the perfect co-star.

✉ INBOX INSIGHTS

July 27

Sue: *"I tend to be guarded and protective in relationships. I'm not the first one to open up about my inner emotions. I don't want to be vulnerable, but there's something so different about getting to know you this way that I feel completely safe. I like that I'm able to let you know how I feel and not wait to get an opening from you. Even though I'm expressing my truth right now, I'm still hoping that it's not too assertive and something that makes you uncomfortable. This is so new to me and I'm testing the waters. I hope that I won't regret hitting the 'send' key."*

July 28

Stephen: *"Thank you for opening up with regard to your feelings. You're not being too assertive, and I really appreciate the risk you are taking. I'm very similar in that I tend to be somewhat reserved at first, opening up when I sense that the feelings are mutual. When I was a teenager, I was very open about my feelings and was often hurt in relationships. It got so that I swore to myself that I would never be hurt again. Now that I'm older, I find that just about everyone has been hurt in the past and that if I don't open myself to the possibilities, nothing will happen."*

California Girls

~ Stephen ~

When I first received Sue's profile, I remember reading it and wondering if I could manage a long-distance relationship. Her pictures intrigued me. She was of a similar age, successful, attractive, and well-traveled—everything I was looking for.

I was still debating on whether to contact her when I received her message about how we were perfectly matched, aside from living on opposite sides of the U.S. However, she also said that if I was ever in California, I should give her a call and perhaps we could meet for coffee.

That encouragement was all I needed to contact her.

Soon enough, we were emailing each other every day, discussing the usual things one talks about when getting to know someone, such as our professional lives, travel, and family. I looked forward to arriving at work every morning. Once I got to the office, I would turn my computer on and get a cup of coffee while it warmed up. I was elated each time I saw an email from Sue waiting for me. I would read it, thinking of her and our relationship, and respond while I drank my coffee. On weekends I would check my email first thing in the morning and send a response.

The geographical distance between us made it easy to be open and share with each other, and we discovered that we had much in common. We decided early on that even if a romantic relationship wasn't in our future—either because of distance or a lack of chemistry when we finally met in person—we would at least remain friends and pen pals.

On the other hand, I wasn't ready to count us out. I was very excited about this budding relationship. Sue was not like the other women I had met online. She was bright, articulate, financially stable, and we had many shared experiences. I felt that I had finally found my soulmate.

One potential problem was our political differences. Sue had indicated that she was a conservative. I was raised in a family with FDR Democrats who believed that the government should work for the people, not to line the pockets of the politicians. So, I addressed my concerns with her directly and was pleasantly surprised when she agreed with me on at least the issues that were most important to me.

Problem resolved. The distance was also a problem, but it was one that could be solved too.

I knew that Sue felt at home in California and didn't think she could relocate, though she wasn't averse to a long-distance relationship that involved alternating visits and traveling together. But I wasn't really tied to Atlanta. My children lived in other states, and I had cousins on both coasts. I believed that with my background and experience, I could write or consult wherever I lived. In fact, I had already been thinking about moving back to Los Angeles to be closer to my younger brother, who had been suffering from Parkinson's Disease for more than 30 years. So, maybe California *wasn't* out of the question for me.

We were getting closer and closer through our emails, and I trusted Sue. I believed she was who she said she was, but given my past experiences, I was happy to receive confirmation from my close friend, Lois.

I've known Lois for more than 50 years (ever since our fathers arranged for us to meet when we were in college in San Jose), and she has lived in the same area as Sue for many years. I texted Lois and told her that I met someone online from Newport Beach and mentioned Sue's name. I was pleasantly surprised when she knew who Sue was, although she didn't personally know her. Then, as fate would have it, she and Sue ran into each other at a local event a week or so later. They spoke while waiting for the valet to get their cars. Lois confirmed the meeting.

I breathed a sigh of relief that Sue was actually a real person. A real person I really wanted to meet *in person*.

✉ Inbox Insights

July 26

Stephen: *"I would like to meet you in person and would like to plan a trip to do so. I've thought about how a cross-country relationship might work and if I would be willing to relocate to California. Have you given it any thought? We seem to have so much in common and have been open and honest in sharing our feelings and thoughts. It would be a shame not to meet."*

Sue: *"For the sake of old-fashioned protocol, I hesitated to make the first move and then decided to hell with it. We're both in our 70s, not in high school and hopefully wise enough to catch something good if it's floating out there. I think what we have so far is great and I agree that we're getting to know each other more than superficially. I really want to take this to the next step by talking and meeting and see what happens. What I find amazing is that this is really 'mature' since we all make judgements based on appearances. This is not the case for us."*

Flame or Fizzle?

~ Sue ~

After two months of this insane correspondence, it was apparent that it was time to meet face to face. Stephen was coming to Los Angeles to visit his ill brother, who lived an hour north of me, and said he'd also make time to visit me. (Months later, he admitted that meeting me was really his primary reason for the trip.)

He planned to stay overnight with his friend Lois and her husband, who live minutes from me, and said he would come to my home late afternoon.

Two days before his trip, he began posting a countdown in his daily email. I knew he was really looking forward to meeting me. The feeling was mutual.

Like any other romantically inclined, overly neat woman, I

made sure the house looked as good as I did. There were the right number of flowers and candles, beautiful towels and soaps in the powder room, a bottle of my favorite Pinot Noir ready to be opened, and a variety of gourmet crackers and cheeses. The lighting was appropriate, the pillows perfectly karate chopped, and my outfit carefully selected, with just enough perfume. No detail was overlooked. I wonder how much of this he even noticed. Men are definitely a different breed.

The doorbell rang. It was time to just "go for it."

As I opened the door, I wondered (not for the first time) whether he would look like his online photo? Well, yes he did, but seemed much shorter than the anticipated 6' and was wearing glasses. That was all OK with me. I immediately thought of all the wonderful attributes he had and the fact that I had been enamored with him for months. So what if he had fudged the numbers a little on his height?

That's when I realized I was standing at the top of the steps and he below. Naturally, he looked shorter. Was it observation or judgement? Regardless, it was all good.

I looked for the dozen roses that I had assumed he would bring me. Instead he was holding one of his famous books, which is commonly used in the scientific world. Yes, he was a scientist and thought like one. He apologized for not bringing flowers but said he hadn't seen a florist. Again, it was all good with me.

We shared a hug that was longer and deeper than the usual friendly greeting. I showed him around the house, and then we sat in the family area, overlooking the ocean, which is always impressive. Conversation flowed easily, and I felt that the evening was off to a strong start.

The plan was for us to have a glass of wine and spend a little time getting acquainted in a non-virtual reality, then head off to dinner. I had made reservations at a romantic restaurant close to my home. The booth was elegant and the service gracious, as was everything about the environment.

It didn't take long for Stephen's alter-ego—the non-scientific part of his brain—to find my hand, which he proceeded to hold tightly for most of the evening. Wine, candlelight, excellent cuisine, and warm words filled the night. I felt confident that this was everything I had expected and a lot more, and I believed this relationship had the potential to be a lasting one.

Dinner that first night solidified what I was thinking and feeling. We already knew so much about each other but found even more to discuss—from the wine he selected, to our families, to politics, to plans for the next few days, to what we both wanted out of the rest of our lives. It wasn't typical first-date banter. We were already way past small talk, so the conversation was filled with depth and anticipation.

The time we spent together while he was in California seemed to fly by. I knew if we were going to continue building on this relationship, we would have to spend more time together. Having traveled extensively, I thought nothing of getting on an airplane and flying to Atlanta to spend time with him on his territory. Being more mature now (older, actually), my inhibitions and concerns about being aggressive no longer mattered. I didn't have another 70+ years to play games and assume any Victorian mores. I wanted to see how it would be to spend time in his world, in his home, and truthfully, I was already missing him. A few days after he left, I called and suggested I reciprocate the visit.

The next three weeks until we would be together again seemed like an eternity. The separation, the absence, was overpowering my senses. I wanted to be in his presence, not kept apart by the width of the country. My feelings intensified.

Those three little words were there, hanging around us like one of those speech bubbles in a comic strip, but they remained unspoken. Stephen and I both knew we were falling in love, but neither of us acknowledged it in our emails or phone calls. Instead we talked about "caring for" and missing each other, how important we had become in each other's lives, and how much we wanted to be together.

It eventually became an unspoken joke, circumventing the phrase "I love you."

✉ Inbox Insights

Sept 3

Sue: *"It's odd, but before last week, it was easier to write about a variety of topics, mostly neutral or questioning and occasionally hinting at some feelings. Now I'm consumed with the feeling aspect and the others we touch on in the calls and texts. Simply put, I miss being with you, care so much, and want us to enjoy what we have right now."*

Sept 4

Stephen: *"I have to tell you that I am amazed at how quickly our relationship is blooming and progressing. I think it's something that we both want very much. Being with you and holding you close just feels right. It's as if it was meant to be. I'm really looking forward to your visit. I'm stocking up on frozen yogurt for you."*

Sue: *"Every day our relationship becomes stronger and deeper and, as you, it amazes me. It's quick, but it is simply right and meant to be. A storybook tale!"*

I Can't Help Falling
in Love with You

~ Stephen ~

Meeting Sue felt like meeting someone I had known for a long time. After dinner that first evening, I had trouble sleeping. I kept thinking of her and how much I had enjoyed our time together, and how much I was looking forward to seeing her the next morning for breakfast.

Our second day together was just as special as the first. After breakfast, we drove to Balboa Island, a beautiful area near where Sue lived and where my family spent summers when I was in high school. We took the ferry across the bay and had lunch at a seafood restaurant in the Pavilion, a structure that was built in the early 1900s. While we ate, I told Sue of my childhood recollections, and after lunch, we walked to the neighborhood where I had once lived. I hadn't been there in years, and memories came flooding back.

That day, we walked more than four miles. My feet were tired, but the company was so great, I didn't mind. It seemed like we never ran out of things to talk about.

By the time the weekend was over, I was beyond smitten, so I was thrilled when Sue offered to come to Atlanta. I couldn't wait to see her, and I knew from our emails that she was feeling the same way I was about our budding relationship. It felt right. She made me feel complete. I had found someone who occupied my thoughts and desires. I felt content and satisfied when I thought of her, and I had high hopes for our future together.

In retrospect, there were some rumblings that were signs of the problems that we would soon face. Sue had told one of her best friends about us the previous weekend. The friend spoke to both of Sue's daughters and voiced concerns about how fast things were moving with us. She didn't want Sue to be hurt since we'd only been together for three days.

To be fair, it was those three days, plus more than a month's worth of emails and phone calls where we had gotten to know each other, where we had shared our most vulnerable thoughts, and where we had begun to fall in love. Still, I understood the friend's concerns and told Sue that she was only looking out for her. Sue assured me that she did not care what others thought and she knew they would love me when they met me.

I had already briefed my children on our relationship. Shortly after I visited Sue, they both came to spend the weekend with me. I told them about my California trip and my strong feelings for Sue, and they were both very happy for me.

Sue and I still talked every other day and maintained the daily emails. I also began texting her before I went to bed, telling her goodnight and sending a virtual kiss. I was feeling so comfortable about our relationship that I cancelled my online dating memberships. I had no interest in meeting anyone else. Thankfully, Sue felt the same way.

I found myself thinking of her all the time. We had a mutual passion for life, and our goals and lifestyles were so much alike. I knew that things were moving fast, but I was OK with that. I felt that time was of the essence at our stage of life and I wanted to make the most of it ... preferably with Sue.

✉ **INBOX INSIGHTS**

Sept 8

Sue: *"I don't remember the last time I was so happy for such a continuous time. There are always fleeting periods of joy, but since you came into my life, the good feelings never leave. It rolls over to other parts of my life."*

Sept 10

Stephen: *"In thinking about our relationship, I think we're at the stage where we're very happy and excited to hear from/talk to/be with each other. We're also sharing our happiness with friends and family. It's great to be with someone who excites you and makes you feel good all over. There is a lot I want to tell you, but I want to wait until I see you on the 22nd."*

The week before her visit, we had a landmark phone call. We talked about things that we both previously thought could only be discussed in person. We were so much in sync, mutually understanding, supportive, and on the same page. I wanted to tell her more about how I felt and to discuss options for dealing with this bicoastal relationship, but I decided to wait until we were together again.

As Sue's visit approached, we exchanged a flurry of short emails. It seemed there was a lot of nervous energy that had to be released. The day of her arrival, I sent an email telling her I would see her in six and a half hours, and to expect a hug and more. Then I ran a bunch of errands and took care of all the grocery shopping. I stocked up on chocolate frozen yogurt and some of her other favorite foods. I wanted her visit to be special and didn't want anything to interfere with our time together.

That afternoon, I left work early to drive to the airport. It was bumper-to-bumper traffic for about 10 miles before I could actually drive at the speed limit. I was getting anxious that her flight would arrive early and that she would be looking for me, but I arrived just in time.

As I parked the car, I received a text from Sue telling me that her fight had landed and that she would meet me by the escalator. I walked quickly to the area where we had planned to meet. People were continually coming up the escalator from the train, but Sue was not among them. The crowd of people thinned out eventually, but still no Sue. Had we gotten our signals crossed? Perhaps she came up the escalator before I got there and was now in baggage claim?

I was concerned that things had gotten off to a not-so-auspicious start. I called Sue, who said she was waiting for me by the escalator. I finally realized what had happened. She was at the escalator that would take her from her terminal down to the train, which would take her to the escalator where I was waiting. About 10 minutes later, Sue appeared and shrugged sheepishly as I walked up to her. I gave her a big hug and a kiss, and then we headed to baggage claim to get her suitcase.

I decided to take a different route home, so I could show Sue the city center. The traffic would be bad no matter which route we took. We eventually arrived at my home, and I had everything planned out. After giving Sue a quick tour of the house, I opened a bottle of Cabernet, poured two glasses, and led her to the couch.

I had something important to say, something I had almost told her in several emails but had resisted, something I had already hinted at during our landmark phone call when I just couldn't resist anymore. But I hadn't officially said those three little words. I wanted the first time to be special, and this felt special enough to me.

I told her that I loved her and that I wanted to spend the rest of my life with her. Even though I had expected her to say it back, I was still relieved when she did.

Next, I took her though each of the options I had been considering, eliminating them one after another. She could move to Atlanta and live with me, but I knew this was a non-starter. Her family, and her place, was in California. I could move to Corona del Mar and buy a home near hers, but that was probably out of the question because of the price differential between homes in Atlanta and homes in Corona del Mar (or for that matter, any nice area in Southern California). The third option was for me to move to Corona del Mar and live with Sue in her house.

That option was the most appealing for Sue, and I was optimistic that we could work everything out. We discussed how we could enlarge her house to make room for some of my things, especially the art and my office. I also decided to put my house on the market ASAP.

The rest of the weekend was almost as wonderful as that first night. It was filled with lots of wine, tasty food, and enjoyable conversation—much of it about our future together.

I didn't want the weekend to end, but Monday eventually came. To avoid traffic, we took MARTA (the train) to the airport. We rode sitting side by side and holding hands. I helped her check in at the airport, and then we said our goodbyes before she went through security.

When I got back home, I felt lonely after the amazing time we had together and walked around my house hoping to find her. I must have been tired as well, because I slept like a rock that night, dreaming of my future life with the woman I loved.

✉ INBOX INSIGHTS

Sept 25

Sue: *"It's easier to be more creative with signing on and off now that the L-word has come out in the open. So many more choices. I slept the duration of the four-hour flight. As I drove up to the house, all I could think about was how we can add that extra room. Then I walked inside and almost hyperventilated figuring out where all your beautiful possessions would fit. I wish you were here to look at it with me and reassure me that it will all work out beautifully.*

Until this weekend, the unknown was 'does he/she love me as I love?' Once that biggie was so happily confirmed, the rest should be easy. As long as we're together, I know it will work out. I am so happy you're in my life. I love you and look forward to years and years of a growing relationship. It will only get better."

Dreams, Drama, and Doubt

~ Sue ~

My trip to Atlanta was everything I'd hoped it would be. Of course, the best part was hearing Stephen say that he loved me and that he wanted to be closer to me, emotionally and geographically. We were both so elated that we almost simultaneously agreed to spend the rest of our lives together. It seemed so right.

Romantic? Yes. Crazy? Even more so. This happened on the fourth day we had spent together ... ever.

He rationalized that at our age, what was the point in waiting? Why waste time? We were mature, sensible adults; at least we convinced ourselves that we were.

It took a few seconds until I bought into the idea of him

relocating for me, but once I decided to drink the Kool-Aid, I gulped it right down. The dreamer in me only saw love and excitement. Nowhere did reality enter the picture during the next few days we were together.

With that out of the way, we enjoyed the rest of my trip. As he showed me around his city, every moment together felt simultaneously comfortable and exciting.

I loved seeing Stephen in his natural habitat. He is the most experimental eater I have ever encountered. He could have his own food show on the Travel Channel. I, on the other hand, have become a very simple and healthy eater. My first night in Atlanta, we went to an Ethiopian restaurant. While we were waiting outside for our table, we walked around, and I kept looking at him thinking he was now part of me and my life. I was in a strange city, at a strange restaurant, with a relatively strange man, and my world was upside down.

I didn't mind a bit.

When it was time for me to go, Stephen took me to the airport, actually checked me in, and made certain I was comfortable before he left. This gentlemanly send-off made me feel protected and cared for, and I relished the thought that I would no longer have to always fend for myself.

As I boarded my plane back to California, I knew that my life as I knew it would never be the same again, and I was ready. It was thrilling, and I was so happy and anxious, at age 76, to begin a new chapter. There were no doubts, no questions, only some logistics to work out.

For example, we had to figure out what to do about Houdini—

Stephen's other love, his Pembroke Welsh Corgi. He told me early on about his devotion to Houdini and how important the dog was in his life. I understood this but couldn't relate. Stephen tried to convince me that Houdini was different from most dogs and was trained at a doggie boot camp. After being with Houdini, I had to agree that he was the best-behaved dog I had ever seen and extremely smart. However, this didn't change my feelings about living with a dog one iota. I had owned dogs when my children were at home, and I like animals, but not enough to change my lifestyle. But given Stephen's love for his dog, it was very meaningful to me when he agreed that Houdini would remain with his ex-wife. Our relationship seemingly had overcome yet another major obstacle, and we kept barreling ahead with our plans for a new lifetime. All was so very good and bright.

We still had other logistical decisions to make, but at the time, I thought that part would be trivial. How foolish of me!

It was nice to be home, but I was sad that I wouldn't see Stephen for another month. Emails, texts, and telephone calls were very weak substitutes for being together, but digital communication would have to do for at least a little longer. Soon enough, we would be together forever.

I walked around in my private love bubble for a little while. Then I decided to share my happiness with the people I love most. And that's when the bubble burst. I anticipated joy, elation, enthusiasm, and questions. Never did I expect the course of events that followed.

Reality hit, and hit hard, when I told my daughters. In my excitement, I reverted to an old pattern which has gotten me into much trouble in the past: over-sharing. It was natural for me to tell people that I had met a man and was ecstatic, and natural for me to give TMI ... too much information.

The huge mistake was in my presentation, particularly with my daughters. One of them asked if I had a good trip, and after telling her how wonderful it was, I blurted out that it was so wonderful that Stephen was going to move in with me, and I was starting a new life.

Within minutes my other daughter was in on the news. What came next was not pretty. Neither of them minced words. I had spent seven days with this man, spread across two weekend encounters, and now I was changing my life. They were disappointed and angry that I would make such plans without even introducing them first. It was all just too fast and not thought through. They said I was acting irrationally and impetuously, which was not like me at all. They reminded me how important personal space was to me and said they couldn't believe I was planning to share the home that was my sanctuary with a stranger. What was wrong with me? One daughter said she believed that she knew the "real" me better than I knew myself in this situation, and that this was not what I would eventually want, especially without doing a trial run. They made it clear they didn't "approve" (which is a surreal thing to hear from your daughters) and said that I should stop what I was doing.

What hit me the hardest was when one daughter told her children, they said they never wanted to stay at my house again if there was some new man living there. How heavy was that? My other daughter wouldn't even tell her children until everything came to fruition. They didn't need to know every detail of the scenario as it was playing out.

I'm blessed to have a fantastic relationship with all six of my grandkids. I adore them, and they are a very significant, central part of my life. I understood that it was the suddenness, the shock that caused this backlash, not Stephen. No one knew him, and I think at that point, they didn't *want* to know him.

I was very defensive and hurt. I wanted my daughters to be happy and excited for me, as I had been for them when they first met the loves of their lives. They knew what I had been through with their father's passing, and it stung that they weren't supportive of my newfound happiness.

The three of us are very close, and suddenly I found the phone contact dwindling. I didn't want to hear what they had to say, and they obviously felt the same way. I was definitely feeling a strong rift in my nuclear family, which is all the family I have. It was another push-pull time in my life. I believed I had a chance for happiness, but I knew I needed my daughters and their families, and it seemed the two weren't possible to have at the same time.

My children are wise and sensible adults. In retrospect, I realize they probably would have been gentler and more supportive if I had done things differently. I should have (famous last words) told them that Stephen and I were very happy together and were considering a long-term relationship. That's *all* I should have said. Details were not important at that point. Indirect intent would have been sufficient. They said I used shock tactics in sharing so much, so soon.

I was shattered, but stubborn, rationalizing, and putting on the proverbial spin.

✉ INBOX INSIGHTS

Oct 5

Sue: *"When we hung up last night, I felt an emptiness. I wanted to be back in Atlanta with you, holding hands with that barely perceptible squeeze, looking into each other's eyes, and have the reassurance that everything will work out well. Being together feels so right, something we both want and know that it is destined to be. Being apart, on the other hand, feels incomplete with tones of unease ... not about us, but about compromise and resolution. I can handle the present situation with my family. I know it will be great once you're a reality to them and not someone I've seen 7 days. That's easy. The part that is so difficult and tearing at me is your family, aka Houdini. The last thing I want is for you to be sad or resentful. I never anticipated this issue and am really distraught. We are so in tune and alike in almost every way, which is the foundation and strength of our relationship and future. I love you very much, and this challenge is a big one, I know."*

Oct 6

Stephen: *"We will get through this as we will every other issue we have to work through. Don't feel distraught. There were always going to be problematic issues that wouldn't be easy to deal with."*

An Uneasy Feeling

~ Stephen ~

*L*ike Sue, I couldn't wait to tell my family about our big plans. As soon as I returned from the airport after dropping her off, I texted with my kids regarding our weekend. When they asked me what we decided, I responded that I would tell them in a phone call. I guess they couldn't wait, because my son arranged a conference call for that evening. They took the news much better than Sue's children.

My daughter emphasized that we are family and that they just wanted me to be happy. I told them that I was *very* happy, and they asked when they could meet my mystery woman. Sue and I had already made plans to do a road trip with my Maserati Club later that month, and we would be passing through Asheville, North Carolina, and Greenville, South Carolina, both of which are just a few hour's drive from my daughter's house in Chapel

Hill. She said she would meet us in Asheville or Greenville, and my son offered to fly down from New York City and join us. I told them I would send them the dates and hotel information and let them decide which place worked best for them. I was looking forward to introducing them to the love of my life.

I was also looking forward to meeting Sue's family, but as I would soon learn, the feeling wasn't exactly mutual. The next morning, there was an ominous sentence in Sue's email about how she received calls from her "sweet, loving, endearing daughters who [she wanted] to kill." I called her later, and she filled me in.

I was a little disheartened, but I told Sue that her daughters probably had her best interests in mind and that I hoped their issues would be resolved before I sold my house and moved to California. Sue appreciated my understanding and said she felt that our conversation reinforced that we were right for each other and were doing the right thing. She believed that once they met me, everything would be fine.

To that end, we discussed meeting in San Francisco in early November. One of Sue's daughters lived in the Bay Area, so I could meet her and her husband. Then I would come to Newport Beach for Thanksgiving, and that would be my opportunity to meet the rest of the family and some of Sue's friends.

In the meantime, Sue had the chance to meet my cousin, Jerry, who went to high school with one of her best friends. The three of them met for lunch, and they got along fabulously. Later, Jerry called me to say how much he enjoyed meeting Sue.

We also continued to discuss the logistics of our new life

together. Sue had lived in her current home for decades, and it held many memories of her previous life. We talked about buying a place together and starting fresh as a couple. Unfortunately, it would not have been an equal partnership, because her current home was worth much more than mine. While I thought a new house would be a great solution for potential space problems, I was uneasy about what would happen if Sue passed away before I did. The house would go to her children, and I might be left homeless and unable to afford a place to live. It seemed that moving into her home was still the best option.

There was still much to decide, and we were emailing and talking on the phone daily. We discussed sharing household expenses and whether we would be OK financially. I thought we would be just fine. I don't believe two can live as cheaply as one, but I believed that sharing expenses would be financially beneficial for both of us in the long run. I hoped that the money we saved could be used for travel, something that we both liked to do.

We also spoke about what I would do in Corona del Mar. I was retired (well, sort of) but remained active, working 30 hours a week, writing and lecturing. There were several universities in Sue's area with programs that were compatible with my expertise and experience. I sent several emails inquiring whether they had openings for a part-time faculty member. I felt confident that the offers would come rolling in.

I also needed to figure out what to do about Houdini, the beloved dog that I shared with my ex-wife. I had him every other day, and we covered for each other when we traveled. Houdini was great company and provided unconditional love. I often found myself talking to him like he was another person.

He would look at me with his large, expressive eyes and cock his head to the side as if he understood everything I was saying.

Leaving Houdini would be difficult for me. It brought back memories of when I moved from Portland to Atlanta for a job at the CDC. I had to tell my then-7-year old son that I was moving, but we would still see and talk to each other. I still remember the tears streaming down his face and wondering if I had made the right decision. Now I would have another difficult decision to make, because Sue was not receptive to having a dog (even a very cute one) in her house. In the end, I decided the sacrifice was worth it for Sue.

Wildfires had broken out in Southern California. I was concerned that Sue's home was in danger from the Orange County fire, but Sue assured me she was still out of the danger zone. From the news reports, I learned that the fires were extensive, and the winds and lack of rain were making them difficult to control.

Sue was safe, but the news still made me feel uneasy. I had grown up in Southern California and experienced the Bel Aire fire in 1961, which came within a block of my home on Sunset Blvd. I can remember my father standing in the front yard with a hose, watering the shingle roof so that it would not catch fire from the burning cinders. It had been several decades since I lived in Southern California, but if I relocated there to be with Sue, I would be trading hurricanes and tornadoes for earthquakes and fires. Compared to leaving Houdini, this was a small price to pay.

Sue seemed to be as excited about our relationship as I was. She was sharing the fact that she was in love with her friends and family. It was not unexpected that some of these individuals were urging caution and told her that things were moving too fast, but I began to worry about their influence on Sue. I was hopeful that things had been smoothed over with her daughters. I felt anxious. I knew that their reaction wasn't due to me *per se*. Nevertheless, I didn't want to be responsible for having a negative effect on Sue's relationship with her family.

Still, I believed that things would work out for the best in the end, and that Sue and I were in a great place. I found myself being more vulnerable with Sue in our communications than I have been in previous relationships, perhaps because her openness and honesty made me want to reciprocate. This strengthened our relationship, and I felt there was nothing that I couldn't tell her. There were no hidden agendas, which made me feel revitalized and more communicative than I have ever felt before.

Around this time, Sue and I started talking about sharing our experience by writing a book together. We discussed what such a book would be like. Sue had a lot of ideas and had printed all our emails and placed them in binders. She started making notes for each chapter. I hadn't started writing because I wanted to wait until we were together for the upcoming "road trip" so we could put an outline together and talk about the chapters.

I didn't suspect that Sue was starting to have doubts. I knew that her daughters and friends were urging her to go slowly, and that she was having second thoughts about our planned living arrangements. Still, I believed we were both in agreement about spending the rest of our lives together. And to increase her level of comfort, I was planning to spend as much time as needed talking about it.

✉ Inbox Insights

Oct 9

Sue: *"I think I'm getting down to writing trivia to you after we speak late at night. The first few months of sharing who we are, what we believe, our pasts, our families, our goals, and eventually feelings led to the relationship we have now. It was so easy to express feelings in those emails, although often circuitous. It was fun reading between the lines. I'm such a Pollyanna that I wanted that to go on forever. Remind me that real life isn't like that and the beauty of the everyday, the familiar, the less intense brings another level. Comfort and companionship and a different love, which we now have and will grow deeper as time goes on."*

Oct 10

Stephen: *"Do you think we're suffering (not literally) from communication overload? We write, text, and talk daily. As you mentioned, we're running short of new things to tell each other and talking about daily mundane things. This is not bad as it keeps us connected with each other's lives and shortens the time between visits. I do agree that we've settled into a new phase. Before we talked about the 'L-word,' each email was intense and scoured for hidden meanings. I think we're in a growing phase now where we are fitting into each other's daily lives. Both are necessary for the long-term development of our relationship. My belief is that the period when we're apart will only strengthen our relationship and deepen our love for one another."*

From Second Chances to Second Guessing

~ Sue ~

My daughters weren't the only ones who were concerned about my recent decision-making. My friends also were a bit uneasy, but being of a similar age, they looked at the situation differently and were gentler with me.

Nobody cared that we'd met online. They were just happy that I'd met someone wonderful. They told me that I was radiant. I looked alive and more vibrant than ever, and I gave off an aura of contentment. They had shared many of my sorrowful times and were delighted that I now had a new chapter beginning.

Still, they advised me to slow down. They felt I was rushing into something that needed time. They also reminded me that my mantra had been that I would never remarry and never live with anyone—I had been adamant about that—and they were worried that I might regret my decision once Stephen was in my home.

They weren't wrong. I was going against everything I had said since I began dating. I have two friends who both had 10-year romantic relationships where they lived separately from their lovers and never married. That's what I had always envisioned for myself, if I found the right man.

Larry had been gone for more than nine years, and although I'd had a relationship with Bob during that time, neither of us wanted to live with anyone, so we had been content with two separate homes. That arrangement worked wonderfully for us, and most of the time, I loved being alone. When I was ill or troubled, I wished there was someone by my side, but most of the time, I enjoyed having my own space.

Why I suddenly thought I no longer wanted that is an enigma. Maybe I was blinded by excitement and adrenaline, or maybe it was just that I didn't see any alternative with Stephen, other than a long-distance relationship, which wasn't what either of us wanted. Our bond was so intense, and I was caught up in a frenzy. Rational thinking had never taken over the wave I was riding, but now it seemed I was crashing into the shores of reality.

Regardless, I pressed forward with our plan, which required more development on my part. No matter how much I was in love, I was still me—a business woman and good with finances. Larry and I had worked long and hard to accrue our wealth, and I was not going to be foolish about giving it away. I brought this up to Stephen, and we agreed that I would meet with my accountant and design a plan that would be equitable and protect both of us. Then we would go to an attorney and have papers drawn up to spell out everything in our agreement. We weren't going to marry, and we wanted to be certain that there were no gray areas regarding the financial aspect of our partnership, during life or when one or both of us passed.

My daughter thought it was quite clinical and more of a business partnership than a loving relationship, but it was both, and I strongly believe that is how it should be.

✉ INBOX INSIGHTS

Oct 12

Sue: *"I admit that our businesslike talks are not pleasant, and I prefer to be blinded and relish in the love part. I'm sorry that I disappointed you tonight and hope that some of the subsequent conversation took the edge off and shone a positive light on what will be. I want to share my life with you, under one roof. When I said that tonight at dinner, jaws dropped. No one could believe my change of heart, but of course they were happy for us. When I talk about you with others, it makes me miss you even more and yearn for the time we'll be together again. It rekindles the feelings and excitement I've had."*

So went the next weeks. I was in planning mode. I was in love and excited about the future. But I was also starting to feel something that I didn't want to feel: doubt.

It didn't help that those closest to me kept questioning what they referred to as my "naïve and rash decision" for Stephen to move to California and into my home. I had been in that house for 21 years, and I loved it. Not only did I have beautiful memories there with Larry, but in the nine years since his passing, I had redecorated everything and made it my own.

I fiercely defended my decision to everyone else, but the truth was that while I didn't want to give up my newfound love, I also didn't want to give up (or share) my home. I'd wake every morning in the bed that had been mine alone for so many years and contentedly begin my daily routine: eat breakfast solo, read the *Los Angeles Times,* and watch the TV news. I'd send and respond to emails, make calls, set up appointments, and leave the house each day and evening with a different destination. In general, I could do whatever I wanted, whenever I wanted. If dinner sounded appealing at 4:00 PM, I'd go for it. If yogurt and granola called to me as a meal, I'd indulge. If I wanted to watch a mindless TV show and fall asleep on the couch until the early morning hours, so be it. No one was around to question my choices, and I didn't want to feel responsible for someone not being content with what I was doing. I loved the free-spirited part of my life.

It occurred to me that when Stephen moved in, all of this would change. Much of my décor, which I had passionately spent years perfecting, would suddenly vanish to make room for his. Could I really do that? Those mornings had tones of "out of sight, out of mind." That doesn't mean I didn't think of Stephen. I thought about him all the time, but those early-morning concerns, and perhaps some hidden fears, had me questioning my choices.

However, as each day progressed, I would read his daily email, send him mine, chat with him on the phone in the evenings, and exchange goodnight texts. With those interactions, the barometer of my feelings rose close to its normal, happy point. I missed him.

This push-pull of the repeating everyday scenarios was creating a slow leak in my illusionary world of certainty. I was counting on the idea that once we were together again, we would pick up where we left off.

Still, I was so torn. The emotions of aliveness and anticipation kept colliding with the cautionary words of my family and friends, which seemed to repeat on a loop in my brain. The uninvited negative demons kept creeping into my head, and I started to do a 180. The thought that maybe I was wrong to make such a rash decision kept gaining momentum, until it was more powerful than the excitement of changing my life.

I played scenario after scenario in my head, and in all of them, I was convincing myself that I wasn't ready for such a drastic change.

SECTION 3

. . . . .

Will We, or Won't We?

Sports Cars and Secrets

~ Sue ~

I've always had an interest in automobiles, particularly sports and vintage cars. My brother shared my interest and inspired me to learn more, and to eventually drive one myself, when he bought a British racing car, a dark green Morgan with the signature brown leather belt circling the hood.

I shared this with Stephen in one of our early emails, before we had ever met in person, and it turned out that cars were another interest we had in common. With this in mind, he wrote:

"I belong to the Southeastern Chapter of the Maserati Club. I just received a notice about the fall event, October 19-22, called the Maserati Percorso and Euro Auto Festival. The event kicks off in the Knoxville, TN area on 10/19 with a beautiful drive to Harrah's Cherokee Casino for lunch. From

there, we head to Asheville, NC, for dinner and a night on the town. There will be an overnight stay in Asheville. On 10/20, there will be another scenic drive, including part of the Blue Ridge Parkway, from Asheville to Greenville, SC. The plan is to stop for lunch and scenic waterfalls along the way. Once in Greenville, there will be a 'fabulous' dinner on Friday night. On Saturday, we will participate in the Euro Auto Festival Concours and the Saturday Euro Festival evening event. There are fun events, and Maserati owners are an interesting group of people. I have to let them know in a day or so if I will be attending. I know this is premature, but is there any interest if things work out between us? I suppose I could reserve a place and hope for the best, or just go alone."

I responded that it was 7:30 in the morning, and I hadn't received any better invitation for that date, yet, so I agreed to go. The wise, cynical comment just flowed out, but it gave Stephen further insight into my lighter side.

I had been looking forward to the road trip and rally for months, but as I arrived for my second Atlanta visit, my heart was heavier than usual, as were my thoughts. I had spent agonizing weeks digging deep inside my psyche and my heart, as well as visualizing this new day-to-day forever life with Stephen. On one hand, it sounded exciting and comforting to have this new world to explore in my senior years. On the other hand, the thought of changing everything about my way of life was terrifying.

I didn't want to make such an enormous error if it wasn't the right choice. I decided the safest thing to do was to live status quo. Maybe there was another way we could be together without him moving into my home. I knew that was what he wanted and what we'd planned, but there had to be an alternative; I just didn't know what it was.

I didn't want to lose Stephen and give up what we had. I felt I was in the middle of a maze, and whichever way I turned, I couldn't get out. The inner conflict was beyond stressful and overwhelming.

I knew I had to tell him that I couldn't go through with our plans before he put his house on the market. I didn't want to disrupt his life more than I already had. I remembered having basically the same conversation with Bob a couple years before, and I dreaded doing it again. I didn't know why I kept rejecting wonderful men. Did I have commitment issues? Was I afraid to be with anyone new? Was I the real-life "Runaway Bride?"

I couldn't (or wouldn't) analyze myself anymore. I just had to brace myself to get the words out. But first we had to participate in the rally.

I decided not to say anything until after the event. I was determined that he would have a great experience and we would share a wonderful time. We do travel well together, which was one of my top criteria in a romantic partnership. Plus, I was genuinely excited about the trip. The entire concept of attending this four-day rally was thrilling—the opportunity for me, a 76-almost-77-year-old woman to participate in an upbeat life that's usually reserved for younger generations. And for all the world travel I'd experienced, there were places in the U.S. I still hadn't visited and wanted to see. These states were on the itinerary. I refused to ruin anything.

Stephen met me at the airport in Atlanta, and it was so nice to see him. He literally whisked me away in his Maserati. We drove towards Tennessee, stopping for dinner along the way, and then began the drive to our first night's stop in Knoxville.

Within minutes, Stephen noted that the tire pressure was rapidly diminishing, until it reached an undriveable level. He barely made it to a service station and tried to repair the damage, but his air pump wasn't working, and I knew we were in trouble. What impressed me was his calmness, since I knew this was a serious problem with a Maserati and the commitment we had to meet up with the group. Stephen showed one slight sign of frustration, not any extreme anger, and no flurry of expletives. It took some creative problem-solving, several phone calls, and the help of a few new friends, but Stephen eventually got us back on the road. I gained great admiration for him and the methodical, well-mannered way in which he handled the problem. Kudos for him.

Early the next morning, we miraculously managed to meet the other members of the Maserati club in time to begin this odyssey. It was like a fairy tale to me. There we were, 10 cars following closely behind one another as we drove through magnificent parks, lakes, forests, and mountains. All the while, heads were turning to view this caravan. It was fall, and the foliage was alive with color. The days were clear and sunny, and the shadows cast were overwhelmingly beautiful. I was awed by the splendor of nature and inspired to take it all in with incredible appreciation. Simultaneously, I loved the juxtaposition of natural beauty with the beauty of man's creation—the intricately designed and executed Maseratis.

Along the way, I felt pride in sitting beside this brilliant man who maneuvered the roads as well as he did everything in his life.

Over the next few days, we traveled through Tennessee, North Carolina, and South Carolina. We ate, laughed, and wined and dined with the other members of the Southeastern Maserati Club, a fun and fascinating group of people. The only thing they all had in common was their love for their cars, so the diversity of the group added to the wonders of the trip. Of course, Stephen and I were the oldest in the group, but we both had friends and colleagues who were much younger, and we never felt uncomfortable about it. I was the odd-man-out since I had never participated with the group before, but Stephen was very inclusive, as were the other members.

Throughout the trip, I acted as best as I could, but later on, Stephen acknowledged that he could feel some distance. In the recesses of my mind, frequently creeping to the forefront, was the knowledge that I had a dreadful deed to do.

The last day of the rally was the European car show, where the array of sports cars was dazzling. The culmination of the trip was an elegant evening. Not only did the food and drinks flow freely, but they also showed movies about cars and a fascinating documentary about Paul Newman. The car buffs loved the technical parts. I, personally, loved to just look at Paul Newman.

The rally experience was perfect, but as it drew to an end, the pit in my stomach got harder and harder to ignore. I knew the start of a great change in our relationship would also begin that night.

When we got back to our hotel suite, I asked him to sit down with me on the couch, so we could talk for a while. He looked me in the eye, and my stomach butterflies were on a rampage.

I tried to tell him as kindly as I could that I couldn't go through with our plans to live in my house, together, for the rest of our lives. I remember trying to lighten the mood by saying that I was "chickening out." I explained that my change of heart had nothing to do with him—I loved him, but I had to live alone.

I wanted him to say something, *anything*, rather than letting me ramble on. But he just stared in disbelief.

I could only imagine all the thoughts that were going through his mind—all the physical moving plans that were in place, the emotion, the letdown, the need to regroup his life. When I questioned him, his response was mostly that he had to digest and process the new situation. He showed no great emotion, but I interpreted it as disappointment on many levels.

I cannot adequately explain how horrible I felt. I've always been ultra-sensitive to other people's feelings, and I go out of my way to do good and show kindness. Now here I was, hurting someone I loved.

The next morning, we didn't dwell much on the topic, and as promised, Stephen drove two hours out of the way to take me to a beautiful gourmet lunch and winery in the countryside. He knew I would love it, and I did, but his kindness only made me sadder.

We drove back to his home in Atlanta and talked a little more about our relationship, and the next morning I flew back to California, knowing the enormous step I had made, questioning the future as it no longer stood. Everything felt unfinished.

I thought I had made the right decision, but had I?

✉ Inbox Insights

Stephen: *"I'm still in a bit of 'shock' after your revelation late Saturday night. I don't think I've entirely processed it and am hoping that by writing about it, I can. I find it easier to express my thoughts in writing than by talking, especially when my emotions are unsettled. I don't want to end our relationship and I know that you don't want to either. My problem is that I built this fantasy in my mind about how my life would be living together. All the things we would do together and the things we would do on our own. It's not easy to recalibrate expectations and feelings. I just hope that the time we will spend together will be sufficient to maintain the feelings that we have for each other. I don't think I can continue to send emails and have phone conversations on a daily basis. I don't know what the optimum is. I suggest we let things settle and see what level of communication is best for our new situation."*

Sue: *"My confusion and disappointment parallel yours. I, too, had fantasies and thought our future together was certain. I had often used the word 'fantasy,' and perhaps that is what it was. I take total responsibility for my presumptuousness and impulsiveness. I think that our age and desires were factors in the quick decision and I didn't want to face reality. I wanted the dream to continue. You are definitely the flexible one, and I am the Pollyanna who wouldn't let herself admit that I couldn't change my way of life. We are at a crossroads as to how we choose to live our lives. Never did I intend to hurt you (and myself). I care so much for you and for the love we share. I love the way we get along, our compatibility, our caring and sharing. The question remains, how do we proceed? I agree that we have to temper the emails and phone calls, although it will truly be withdrawals. I know I'll keep checking constantly."*

Changing Lanes

~ Stephen ~

Like Sue, I had been looking forward to the rally for months. More so, I was looking forward to the road trip and spending time with her. When I met her at the airport, the sight of her made my heart skip a beat.

The trip got off to a bumpy start, literally. I stopped for gas near Chattanooga, Tennessee, and when re-entering the highway, I drove over a rough patch of road. I felt a strange sense of foreboding, and suddenly my tire pressure gauge lit up, indicating a rapid drop in tire pressure. I slowed down, cursing to myself. This was the last thing that I needed.

I eased the car down the road another mile or so to the next exit and then into a gas station. Upon inspection, there was a slit in the sidewall of the left, front tire. It was ruined. We were in the middle of nowhere, and Maseratis do not come with spare tires. To make matters worse, the front tires are a smaller size than the rear tires, and all the tires are unidirectional. So, I didn't just need a new Maserati tire. I would have to find a left, front tire.

Thankfully, there were members of the Maserati Club who lived nearby. I quickly called the one I knew best and explained my situation. He contacted the head of the service department at the Maserati dealership in Knoxville, who said they could replace the tire the next morning. I just had to figure out how to get to Knoxville on three tires.

By then, it was late at night and my options were limited, so I went into a nearby service station and purchased a can of tire sealant. I had a portable tire inflator in the trunk that plugged into the cigarette lighter; however, the cigarette lighter had been co-opted when the radar detector/laser jammer was installed. Therefore, I had no way of using the tire inflator.

While I was getting more frustrated by the minute, Sue went into the gas station and found someone who was willing to let us use her cigarette lighter. Finally, we were able to seal the tire and fill it with enough air so that I could drive, albeit slowly, the 20 or so miles to the hotel in Knoxville.

I breathed a sigh of relief when the hotel was in sight and once again when I parked near the front door. We had only been in our room for a few minutes when my friend from the Maserati Club called to say the dealer did *not* have a left, front tire in stock and would have to order one. It seemed like the weekend was doomed before it had begun.

I thought we would have to stay in Knoxville until the dealership found a tire. However, all hope was not lost. A call went out to Maserati Club members in the Knoxville area, and one member responded that he had an extra left, front tire that was almost new. We arranged to meet him and the tire at the Maserati dealership the next morning. Since he was the president of the Maserati Club, he said that the other cars going on the road trip would wait for us, so we could all drive to Asheville together.

With that behind us, things were looking up at last ... or so I thought.

Even though we had a wonderful time on the trip, I felt that something was amiss. Normally Sue is very chatty, but she was more reserved and quiet, which left me a bit puzzled. However, I attributed it to being with an unfamiliar group of people and jet lag. I certainly had no idea what was coming.

When Sue told me that she didn't want to change her lifestyle and live together in California, I felt like I had been kicked in the gut. My stomach was churning, and I could see all the plans we had made passing before my eyes. Everything her daughters had said about her jumping into a relationship too soon was coming true.

When Sue asked if I had any comments, I could have responded, but I wanted to think things over first. I needed to process what she had just said.

I had a tough time sleeping that night. I didn't know whether I was feeling anger, resentment, or disappointment about how my life had changed so quickly. Maybe it was all three. Either way, I knew that I had to re-evaluate our relationship. Sue had said that she still wanted to have a relationship, but I wasn't sure we could make it work. I didn't want to live on opposite sides of the country and see each other sporadically. I believed that being together would reinforce the special feelings we had for each other, and that being apart most of the time would cause the feelings of love to slowly dissipate into friendship.

I felt a bit awkward being with Sue the next day and was quiet at first. I was still thinking about what she had said the night before and wasn't ready to talk much about the future. To make matters worse, I felt a cold coming on.

Sue emailed me when she got home to California. She mentioned that she had spent the return flight trying to process what she did and restructure our relationship in a way that's a win-win for both of us. She didn't want to lose what we had.

Neither did I, but I was no longer feeling very hopeful about our long-term potential.

I didn't sleep much that night because of my cold, so I got up early the next morning and decided to respond to Sue's last email. I told her how I felt, that I still wanted to spend time together, and that I hoped that time would be sufficient to maintain the feelings we had for each other.

That was true. I did *hope,* but I also had serious doubts.

First things first, I would need to deal with my hurt feelings, which meant I needed to slow down our communication for a while. Later that day, I cancelled both of my flights to California—the one where I would meet Sue's daughter in San Francisco and the one at Thanksgiving when I would spend the holiday with Sue's family and friends.

It was Sue's suggestion to cancel the trips, but we both agreed it was necessary. However, I felt that by doing so, I was beginning to distance myself from her. I was also hurt that she no longer wanted me to be there. It felt like an even bigger break than when she told me she didn't want to live together. If I was still going to be part of her life, why couldn't she share me with her family? Wouldn't they want to meet the person she planned to spend time with, even if we weren't going to be living together? I assumed that Bob had met her family and was present at family functions, so shouldn't I have been afforded the same opportunity?

Coupled with the disappointment that we weren't going to spend our remaining days together, I felt that I was being minimized in Sue's life.

Adding salt to the wound was the fact that I had told my friends and family I would be putting my house on the market and moving to California. This was something else I had to deal with after Sue decided she didn't want to live together. I had even told my neighbors. The neighborhood holiday party was supposed to be held at my house that year, so I had to let them know I would be moving soon. Of course, now I wasn't. I knew my kids would understand and that my brother would be disappointed that I wasn't moving to California. The one silver lining was that I hadn't mentioned any of this to my colleagues at work, so I would at least be spared the embarrassment of telling them about the change in plans.

Now I just needed to figure out what the new plan was.

✉ INBOX INSIGHTS

Oct 28

Sue: *"So, here we are, a week later and I'm feeling very uneasy and haven't been able to understand where we are in our relationship. The clinical emails are so different and don't reflect feelings in any way. Can you share what you're thinking? Do you want to talk or just write? I feel uncomfortable, and that's never been an emotion between us. I don't know where I stand with you. I know I miss you and also know that my revelations were a surprise (actually to both of us) and you needed time to process. So?"*

Oct 29

Stephen: *"I guess that I'm feeling unsettled as well. I thought that I had found the woman I would spend the rest of my life with, only to learn that she doesn't want to live together. I'm at a place where I don't know what to do. Do I spend time with you when I can or do I start to look for someone who wants to be with me all the time? If the former, then what do we do in between being together? I am not lonely, nor am I desperate. But I am not getting any younger. I believe I have a lot to offer and want to share what time I have left with someone that I love and cherish"*

✉ INBOX INSIGHTS

Oct 29

Sue: *"The last four months have been a dream for me, and I 'drank the Kool-Aid.' You so captivated me that I never stopped to face reality and ask what I truly wanted and could have. The answer, of course, was you. Then I dug deeper and found that while my heart was dictating my decisions, the objective part of my brain was being completely ignored. I've learned a lot, which is that after so many years alone, it's become an ingrained way of life, and as much as I thought I could change because of you (us) I can't. My ideal situation would be to have separate homes yet spend much time together. Why did I fall in love with someone 3,000 miles away, which negates both of our needs? The question is, where to from here?"*

The Saga Continues

~ Sue ~

Even though I was the one who threw a wrench in our future plans, the next few weeks and months were tough on me, too, albeit in a different way.

Not only did I miss Stephen and feel extremely guilty about hurting him, but I also felt embarrassed. In my zeal to share my overflowing love with countless friends and family members, I hadn't anticipated that my fairytale would go up in a puff of smoke. We were no longer going to live together: we were no longer the magical couple who was different than everyone else who met online and fell in love through emails. We weren't going share that "happily-ever-after, until we are old and feeble" story.

In addition to family and close friends, I had told members of various groups to which I belonged. I had spoken to realtors about helping Stephen sell his house in Atlanta. I'd told my attorney, accountant, contractor, etc., etc. It almost seemed that I had this need to share my happiness with *everyone*. (I did stop short at telling the checkout clerk at the supermarket who routinely asked about my day. I did have a little filter, even if it was kinda faulty.)

Knowing that most people thought my quick decision to move in with Stephen was impetuous and foolish, I was humbled and embarrassed to admit that things hadn't worked out as I had declared they would. I learned that several different groups of friends had wagers about the lasting power of my proclamations. Some close friends shared an "I knew it" with me, while others merely had that knowing look of "really?!"— which compounded my awkwardness.

I was very uncomfortable, knowing that my whirlwind romance was the topic of negative discussions. At first I put energy on this, which of course, gave it more life and created more gnawing feelings. After a while, people came to accept what was happening, and except for an occasional "tsk, tsk," it was taken for granted. I really am not a major part of their lives, and the saga of my adventure quickly took a backseat to their own drama.

Soon, only a few close friends asked what was happening. Did Stephen and I still write or talk? Did we plan to be friends? With my family, I would casually mention that I still was in contact with Stephen, but never again was a word uttered about the original move-in-forever plan. It was as if it had never happened.

I didn't take long to realize that this adventure with changing my relationship with Stephen was just a few stitches in the pattern of my life, and that instead of beating myself up about what happened, I should focus on the positive impact I have made, the love I have shared with people, and the fact that I have no power over their thoughts, good or bad. I decided I would continue to live my life as the person I am, not one whom others would like or expect me to be.

Put simply, that's when I decided other's opinions no longer held a mirror in which to see myself. It took me 77 years to get there, but I've got to tell you, it feels damn good. Even now, when I reflect on this period in my life, I like to acknowledge the lessons I learned and the growth that still continues, despite my age.

While I didn't care much about what others thought, I did care about fixing things (as best as I could) with Stephen. We never officially "broke up." We transitioned, but not easily. How do you go from a summer of euphoria, to changing the rules of the game and not establishing new ones? That's what seemed to happen. We both processed the change in plans to live together, but neither of us really knew what to do next. We thought we could still maintain a deep friendship, see each other, and travel together. But there was no reset button on this relationship.

The emails slowed down, and the loving goodnight texts vanished completely. We were in a state of flux. We needed to decide on a new normal, whatever that meant for us. And we needed to do it in person.

Of course, we had already cancelled our Thanksgiving plans. That was a tough decision, and I knew that it hurt Stephen's feelings. We had decided to remain close friends, and I really wanted that to be true. But how could I bring him to meet my daughters and to our annual Thanksgiving dinner, knowing he wasn't going to be part of the family? That would be uncomfortable for everyone.

What I still planned, and hoped he'd agree, was that he would come out for Christmas and we would go to Palm Desert, just the two of us. We could use this private time to enjoy each other and make sense of our new relationship, away from all family and friends.

But I didn't want to wait until December to see him again. Stephen agreed, and we planned for me to come visit him in Atlanta. I would arrive on November 12 and stay three days.

✉ INBOX INSIGHTS

Nov 10

Sue: *"We talk about how difficult a long-distance relationship is, and I know it's true. But suddenly it's only two days until we'll be together again. This isn't blinding me, but rather it's a reminder of the speed at which days and weeks pass, especially the older we get. That's a two-edged sword. Regardless, I'm looking forward to seeing you again soon."*

Stephen: *"I, too, have noticed how fast time passes as we get older. I can remember being in grammar school wondering how long it will be until summer begins. The days seemed to just crawl by. I know that there are still only 60 seconds in a minute and 60 minutes in an hour, so time itself doesn't change. However, one's perception of time does. Time seems to just fly by now. I can't believe that we'll be together again in just one day (actually 29 hours)."*

When Stephen picked me up at the airport, he told me that his friends and neighbors had invited us to join them for dinner early that evening. In keeping with Stephen's passion for foods that were new and extreme to my tastes, we went to a highly touted, rather exotic Asian restaurant. I cannot even fathom what he and his friends ordered, but I was cautious with my order and content with the results.

The couple were interesting, charming, and very welcoming. Once again, it was so easy to be together, even with others around. Sitting next to him, I realized how much I had missed him.

The woman is a renowned artist, and Stephen has a magnificent stained-glass window that he commissioned her to create. I was intrigued, so the next day we went to their home and studio and spent a few hours exploring her talents and handiworks. I felt at ease, as before.

Even though the glow had diminished and our plans had changed, our level of comfort continued very high. In fact, we ended up doing something that an old married couple would do. My washer and dryer had broken right before I left home, and I was scrambling to buy a replacement. Stephen gallantly suggested we go to Home Depot in Atlanta, purchase what I needed, and have it delivered from their California warehouse. That way, it would be waiting for me when I got home.

Trite and mundane, I know, but it exemplified the level of familiarity and comfort we had established. It also hinted at the sadness I felt that we were no longer going to be life partners.

One of the beautiful parts of the trip was the two visits we made to his ex-father-in-law, Leonard, who is 102 and as sharp as they come. We got along so well, I joked to Stephen that I had a crush on him. Leonard told Stephen he wanted to take me out, so there was another very warm connection.

When Stephen and I were alone together, it felt great, and when we were with others, it was equally as good. He loves to cook—a talent and interest I lack—so one of our evenings together, he decided to cook some complicated dish he had seen in the newspaper. I, of course, encouraged it and did my part by sharing a glass of wine with him in the kitchen, washing some vegetables, and insisting we feast in his formal dining room, where I set the table and lit the candles. This is something bachelors, even those who cook, don't generally do for themselves. It was a lovely night.

This was all well and good, but my reason for the visit was to gain clarification about the status of our relationship, and I'd told him so in advance. The rest I considered delightful, but trappings.

We didn't make any plans for the future, but I did ask Stephen where we stood—what he thought would happen, how we could create new parameters, and whether he wanted to continue as is. His response was that we'd have to wait and see, which I thought was rather noncommittal and safe, and admittedly a little frustrating. I knew he wasn't playing games with me and was probably still somewhat angry and hurt, but he also knew how honest I am with my feelings. I felt in limbo, not being able to talk about our situation or get any insight from him.

He had already hinted that he would probably find a new life without me, which would satisfy his need to be with someone. I knew this was the consequence of *my* change of heart, not his. It hurt, but I understood. I just didn't know if that had already happened or if he was actively pursuing a relationship with someone else. I didn't get much clarification on that either.

I returned to California, but I couldn't bring myself to stop writing to Stephen, and he continued writing to me. It was more than habit. We had made a deep impression on each other and didn't want to face that emptiness or sever contact, but the contents of our emails were more about the day-to-day happenings in our lives, with fewer mentions of our emotions. It felt like the honeymoon stage was over, and we were a couple who had worn out the intensity of sparks and settled into the comfortable zone.

Only, we *weren't* a couple now. What were we? I still wanted to know myself.

✉ Inbox Insights

Dec 1

Sue: *"Since July, my life has been a series of varying emotions. I'm no longer the person I was before I met you. I was moving along smoothly, with a very full and rewarding life, missing only the major component of a long-term, meaningful, loving relationship. Then there was you and then there was us, full of excitement, hope, and dreams. Now, that has unraveled, and we both have had to process and adjust. The only constant is change, and as I wrote the other day, I have recently discovered that I don't accept it as well as I have before."*

✉ INBOX INSIGHTS

Dec 2

Stephen: *"I appreciate your openness about your feelings. When you told me that you couldn't live with anyone, I had to take time to process the information and decide what I was going to do. I didn't think that I could afford a place to live in Southern California that was comparable to what I currently had. The homes in the retirement communities I looked at online were pretty but about half the size of my current home and for about the same price. It doesn't look like I will be moving back anytime soon. So, the next thing I did was decide whether I would be satisfied with just seeing you periodically. To be honest, I don't know if that is what I'm looking for in the long-term. For the moment, Houdini fills that need. However, I miss the discussions, companionship, and passion that an everyday relationship brings. I guess what I am trying to say is that I will be looking for that in the future. I believe you said that this was one of the consequences of your previous decision. In the meantime, I will work on the book and look forward to our next get-together."*

A Blue Christmas

~ Stephen ~

*T*hanksgiving came and went. Because of the recent changes in our relationship status, I felt a loss and was sad. As it stood, I would remain a stranger to Sue's family. A secret that she was not sharing with them. However, despite everything, I had no regrets. I enjoyed getting to know Sue, as well as the time we spent together. I hoped we could continue the relationship in some way.

Christmas was coming soon, and I looked forward to spending it in Palm Desert with Sue. I wanted to see my brother, Michael, in Los Angeles, so I asked Sue if we could spend a few days in Corona del Mar before heading to Palm Desert. She agreed. The trip turned out to be a prescient decision, as Michael was in the hospital by the time I arrived in California.

A couple weeks before my trip, I received several emails (during the night) from my brother's advocate. She told me that Michael had developed bed sores, and because they were not being treated appropriately by the visiting nurse, they had become infected. Consequently, he was taken to the emergency room at Kaiser Permanente Hospital, where they put him on intravenous antibiotics and debrided the wounds.

I was really concerned about his declining health. Apparently, he could no longer get up and move about, so he sat (or laid) in the same position all day, which is how he had developed bed sores. That coupled with the Parkinsonian dementia made me think that he would not last much longer. I missed my brother and wished that I could talk with him more often. However, his condition made it hard to understand him on the phone, and his dementia meant that he often didn't know who I was. I was frustrated with dealing with this from a distance and felt depressed that there was so little I could do for him.

A couple of days before I was to leave, I received a call from Michael's advocate, saying he was back in the hospital. His caregiver had found him unresponsive and not breathing that morning and called the paramedics. By the time they arrived, he had started breathing again, so they took him to the hospital to determine what had happened. After an initial assessment, he was transferred to Kaiser Permanente Hospital.

When I arrived at LAX, I picked up a car and went straight to the hospital. Michael was still unresponsive. His children, one of our cousins, and Dexter (one of his caregivers) were with him. The news was not good. Michael had suffered a hypoxic event, meaning his brain had been deprived of oxygen for too long, and they were waiting on a neurological examination to determine the extent of the brain damage.

I stayed for a while and then drove to Corona del Mar to Sue's house, with Michael still on my mind. I had wanted this trip to be a happy time when I could rekindle my relationship with Sue. Unfortunately, I was not able to be in a cheerful mood.

The next day, Sue and I met my friends, Lois and David, for breakfast and then drove to Los Angeles to visit my brother. Sue thought I should be with my family, so she stayed in the waiting room and read while I went to Michael's room. I entered the room at the same time as the neurologist, who said Michael had lost higher brain function during the hypoxic event and that it was unlikely he would ever regain what he had lost.

We were all in tears. Even though we knew that Parkinson's is a fatal disease, none of us were ready to lose him. Michael had stubbornly fought its ravages for more than 32 years. We knew how much he enjoyed life and would not want to spend the rest of his days unconscious with a feeding tube.

Michael's kids and I hugged each other and then discussed various options and the prognosis. We thought hospice might be an alternative, but before we made that decision, we asked for a second opinion. It would take a few days to schedule the necessary tests.

We went down to the waiting room, where I introduced them to Sue. They were on their way to get something to eat, so Sue and I left. My mind was occupied with thoughts of my brother and nostalgia for our childhood together in Los Angeles. So, I took Sue on a tour of the homes that we lived in growing up and provided a running commentary of the memories that came rushing back to me.

Michael and I had been close as kids. When we were growing up, we had our disagreements and fights, but I would not let anyone else pick on him. After all, I was the older brother, and it was my job to protect him. As adults, we had become even closer, despite the physical distance between us. And now I was preparing to lose my oldest friend.

The next day was Christmas. I spoke with Adam about Michael's condition. There had been no change during the night. I told him that I would be in Palm Desert for the next few days but could be reached by phone. I would return to the hospital if needed.

On the drive to Palm Desert, I tried keeping things light, but I was feeling sad and conflicted. I knew there was nothing I could do for my brother but still felt I should be at the hospital for his kids. But I also didn't want to disappoint Sue by canceling our vacation plans.

Our time together in Palm Desert went by quickly. Sue was cognizant of what I was feeling about my brother's condition. I really didn't want to talk about our relationship and where it was heading because my level of optimism was at an all-time low.

I spoke with my brother's son a couple of times a day. The results of the second neurological evaluation indicated that my brother would remain basically unresponsive. This was not the quality of life he would have wanted, so his kids decided (and I agreed) to take him home, where hospice nurses would provide palliative care. The doctors said he wouldn't last long without a feeding tube.

I wanted to see him again, so that Friday, I said my goodbyes to Sue, picked up a rental car at the Palm Springs airport, and drove back to Los Angeles. I went to his home and spent some time with him before going to a hotel for the night. When I returned the next morning, I found that his caregiver, Dexter, was excited because Michael had opened his eyes, squeezed his hand, and smiled at him. We called his son to tell him the news. Perhaps Michael would defy the odds and make a recovery.

His children, my cousins, and I gathered in Michael's room. We called his doctor and made the decision to take him off hospice care and return him to the hospital for further tests. For the first time since the call from his advocate, I felt there was some hope.

It would take a few days to get an update, so I returned to Atlanta the following day. A couple days later, my nephew called to tell me that the improvement in Michael's condition was only transient. There was no change in his neurological assessment, so he was returning home to hospice care. His doctor said that he would pass in a few days, a week at most, but he didn't know how stubborn my brother was. Michael lasted almost a month without food or water.

During that time, his son and I arranged to have a FaceTime call each evening during his visit with Michael. Supposedly, hearing is the last sense to go, so during our call, I would read to him the letters that he had sent me and our mother when he was in the Peace Corps, and afterwards when he was traveling through Europe and Israel. His son learned a lot about his father during those calls.

The third week in January, I had a trip to Indonesia to take part in an anthrax workshop sponsored by the U.S. State

Department. I didn't know if my brother would survive that long, but I informed the organizers of the workshop of Michael's situation and made plans to cancel if he passed before I left or return early if he should pass while I was gone. I told my brother that I was going to Indonesia and spoke to him while I was there.

I returned to Atlanta on January 25. Adam called me the evening of January 31 to tell me that Michael had passed away. I immediately called Sue to tell her what had happened and that I would be flying to Los Angeles the next day. Sue thought I should be with family during this time, and I agreed. The funeral service would be streamed live, and Sue said she would be watching.

I wanted to see Sue while I was in town but felt that I needed to help Michael's children with funeral arrangements and with my brother's estate. The status of my relationship with Sue was not on my mind at this time. All I could think about was how much I would miss my brother.

✉ INBOX INSIGHTS

Feb 2

Sue: *"The service was lovely, and your speech was so warm and heartfelt. I hope you all will have comfort with your beautiful memories and the wonderful times you shared. I hope you can sleep on the flight home and take it easy this weekend. You really need to take time for Stephen and be good to yourself now."*

April 2

Sue: *"Our lack of regular emails has created distance. My last email to you was Valentine's Day, and I haven't heard back. That's absolutely fine, but being an organized person and accustomed to writing to each other daily, I'd feel more comfortable knowing what was going through your mind. Do you just want to email when you have something you want to say, rather than a preconceived time? If that's the case, I won't look for emails from you but will be pleasantly surprised when I receive one."*

The Second Time at My Doorstep

~ Sue ~

Obviously, Christmas with Stephen wasn't the holly, jolly experience I had planned. No matter how we tried to be light and find joy, he was living with visions of his very sick brother and the knowledge that Michael's passing was imminent. Stephen tried to engage with me and enjoy our time together, but I could clearly tell that only a small part of him was with me. Emotionally and digitally, he was connected to Michael's children and his cousins.

I absolutely supported his decision to leave early to be with his family, but I was disappointed that we had not had the chance to talk much about our relationship. We had already agreed that we had a very special bond and would be in each other's lives forever, just not under the same roof. However, I wasn't sure exactly what that meant in practice, and I'd hoped to get more clarity during his visit.

In a way, I did. Even before his brother's condition took a turn for the worse, Stephen had planned to fly back to Atlanta on New Year's Eve, as opposed to spending it with me. I admit, I was very disappointed, and I considered it a message. Maintaining our new relationship—which I thought would be a lifelong, close friendship—didn't seem to be as important to Stephen as it was to me. His unspoken choice was loud and clear.

Over the next six months, my contact with Stephen dwindled. In the past, he had made frequent trips to Southern California to visit his ailing brother and his family. Unfortunately, with Michael's passing in late January, those trips lost their regularity.

During the first half of 2018, he made an overseas trip that required preparation, and I knew he was still in the grieving process. The space between his communications grew longer and longer. I understood, and when we did write, he always explained how busy he was. At no point did I feel that he was out of my life, but I was beginning to feel that he wasn't in it either. Obviously, we weren't an active couple, and no steps were taken to see each other again as friends.

My life was busy too. I was still speaking to groups, promoting my other two books, working on this one, involved in finances, and socializing a lot, although not dating. There was a flood in my house, and I spent six weeks living in a hotel, going back and forth to my home, making decision after decision, and wearing myself out. I didn't pine over Stephen and accepted the fact that his place in my life had diminished.

Still, we had agreed to write this book together, and as I was writing about our relationship from my perspective, I realized there was one little problem. The book had no ending. I was still unclear on exactly what was happening with us, so it would be impossible to explain it to our readers.

Clearly, we needed to talk ... preferably in person.

In May, in one of our few-and-far-between emails, I accused him of going MIA. He wrote that he was planning to come west to see his family, so I invited him to spend a few days with me, and he accepted.

Why not? We had proclaimed we would always be friends and share something special, so why not test it out?

The timing was perfect for rekindling relationships. Jerry, Stephen's artist cousin, was displaying his works at a very fine restaurant in Brentwood, and I felt it would be nice to support him. Our mutual friend, Patsy, and her husband, Arnie, graciously hosted Jerry and me to be part of the scene. So, here I was, once again, having a meal with Jerry and Patsy while awaiting a visit from Stephen.

Déjà vu.

Only this time, the anticipation didn't include butterflies. It was filled with conflicting thoughts and nervous energy. How would this all turn out?

On the afternoon of Friday, June 15—nearly a year since we first connected online and 10 months since our first meeting— Stephen once again rang my doorbell, and it was a familiar sight. I looked for the flowers as any romantic would do, but I suppose he never got my first message. But he brought himself cross country to see me; that was enough.

We spoke for a while and then went to a top-rated restaurant, Marche Moderne, the same restaurant where I had planned to take him during his Thanksgiving visit, before I turned everything upside down.

The ambience and dinner were perfect, but I wasn't interested in small talk. I told him it was essential to me that we clearly define the vague relationship. Where did we stand? What did he want and expect? A "let's wait and see when the visit is over" wasn't acceptable to me. Yes, we could revisit this then, but in the meantime, where were we?

Stephen said he was still very interested, cared for me, and could visualize seeing each other more often and traveling together. I felt it was a good beginning, but I also knew we really wouldn't know right then, and I didn't know how I felt about any of it.

The search for closure continued ...

The next few days were full. To make up for the disappointment and hurt I had caused by not bringing Stephen into my family fold, I planned to get together with friends as much as possible while he was in town.

Saturday morning, we had a lengthy breakfast with one of my closest friends and her husband. Stephen was quiet during the meal, and I simply accepted it. That night, we had dinner with his friends of 50 years, whom I had heard about but never met. They were exceptionally bright and interesting. Of course, they all reminisced, played career geography, and discussed their former scientist colleagues—who was ill, who had won prestigious awards and prizes, and who had passed away. They were sophisticated and well-bred, effortlessly including me in the evening. Stephen seemed quite content.

Sunday was Father's Day, and we both spoke to our sons and sons-in-law, starting off the day on a high note. My dear friends were hosting 17 people for brunch at their new, magnificent hilltop home, and I brought Stephen with me. The group was very hospitable and open, and Stephen had a good time. The host is exceedingly bright and accomplished in medicine and science, so he and Stephen spent time together.

I was relieved that Stephen wasn't having difficulty and had found at least one person with whom he could easily relate, although he appeared to be more reserved with everyone else. I hadn't seen him in social situations before, other than with his friends, so I was seeing another, more introverted side of him.

More was to come. That evening, I had arranged for dinner aboard an electric boat with Lois and David. It was an evening full of laughs as we took turns steering the craft through magnificent Newport Beach Harbor, viewing world-class homes and yachts, including John Wayne's house and his impressive boat, "The Wild Goose."

Stephen was our captain for most of the time, and he kept the boat straight and steady. Then I took over while he ate, and control was the last thing I had. We avoided hitting ferries, mega yachts, buoys, small boats, and kayaks ... but only barely. The three of them were hysterical with laughter at my poor boat driving skills, and even I enjoyed the erratic turns. I was surprised (and thankful) that I never hit anything.

I gladly turned the wheel back over to Stephen after he finished his meal, and this time I appreciated his serious demeanor, quietness, and concentration. All in all, it was a great night on the water.

We stopped for dessert on the way home. When we got back to my house, I reopened the conversation about where we now stood and where we would head ... alone or together. I wasn't going to have a repeat of the last time we parted. Stephen reiterated that he still enjoyed being with me and wanted to continue on this path.

I went a step further and acknowledged that we would probably never have more than this wonderful friendship and that there was no long-term future for us. He agreed.

So, it was now out in the open, and most importantly to me, it was clearly understood between us. Early on in our correspondence, he said that no matter how our romance played out, we'd always have the chemistry of friendship, and he was right.

Stephen flew back to Atlanta the next morning, and I said goodbye at the doorstep where we had twice said hello, not knowing when we'd see each other again.

From MIA to TBD

~ Stephen ~

Sue was right about me being MIA for the first half of the year. It wasn't that I was ignoring her, but my brother's passing left a hole inside me. I just didn't have the energy or desire to continue the daily emails. So, they became sporadic and mostly dealt with newsy rather than personal matters.

During this time, I buried myself in work and in helping my nephew and neice settle their father's estate. I took on the responsibility of transferring Michael's share of the land we had inherited from our parents to his children At the same time, I planned to gift my share of the land to my children. I contacted the Mohave County Landowners Association in Kingman, Arizona, and got the name of an attorney who could handle the transfer, and I began to send him the necessary documents.

Sue's email in May was the impetus I needed to schedule another trip to Los Angeles. I hadn't seen Sue or my family since Michael's funeral at the end of January, and I wanted to be with family and friends again. My cousin, Jerry, wanted me to see the paintings he had on exhibit as well. So, I eagerly hopped a flight to sunny California.

It was great to be with Sue again. In fact, I was so excited about seeing her that I completely forgot about bringing flowers. *Mea culpa.* As I pulled up in her driveway, I thought of the day 10 months earlier when I first met her. It was *Déjà vu* all over again.

I really appreciated the effort Sue made to introduce me to her friends. I know she thought I was quiet during that first breakfast, but with all the talking that the two ladies were doing, it was hard to get a word in edgewise. I was OK with that. I just enjoyed seeing her in her natural habitat.

I knew going into the trip that Sue wanted to know where our relationship stood. To be honest, I really didn't know. I had truly believed that Sue was everything I wanted in a partner and in a friend. The disappointment I felt about her not wanting to live together still lingered. So did my doubts that we could be anything more than friends. I could not afford to relocate to Corona del Mar, where I would be close to Sue and where we could see if things worked out. And I didn't think a 3,000-mile cross-country relationship would last.

I still don't, but I believe our friendship is solid and has lasting potential. I will always cherish the time we spent together and will look forward to seeing her during my trips to California. I still plan on traveling together. I haven't been to as many countries as Sue has, so some of the trips may be repeats for her. But that just means I'll have an excellent guide.

In the end, I don't regret my relationship with Sue. While it didn't have a particularly happy ending, it taught me a lot about myself and what I wanted in a partnership. Sue's openness enabled me to be more open and to freely discuss feelings without any fear. This necessitated that I drop the barriers I had erected when I was younger to prevent me from getting hurt. I don't know whether this newfound vulnerability only extends to my relationship with Sue, or if it's something I will be able to replicate in the future. Either way, I feel stronger because of it.

I also learned that I wanted a relationship with someone who was closer to me geographically, someone who could spend more time with me and who would be there for me if I needed any help, and vice versa. While phone calls, emails, and texts are nice, they do not take the place of communicating in person.

Perhaps most importantly, my experience with Sue made me realize that age is not a hindrance to having a loving and fulfilling relationship.

I am still online looking for that perfect relationship. The more I look, the more I realize that there may never be a "perfect" person for me. People our age have a lifetime of experiences and relationships that have shaped who they are today. When two people are "set in their ways," change is an impediment that must be overcome. I guess I'm coming to grips with the fact that I will have to prioritize what's important to me in a relationship if I'm to find happiness.

In the meantime, I have a lifelong friend and travel buddy in Sue. Even though our love story didn't turn out like I had hoped, I believe there are still new chapters for us to write, and those will have a happier ending.

Epilogue

~ Sue ~

Man plans and the universe laughs.

Thus goes the paraphrasing of an expression I heard from my grandmother when I was a toddler. When a wise friend repeated these words to me recently, it struck me that there is an amazing truth in that simple but powerful sentence, and my relationship with Stephen has been yet another example of how little control we really have over fate.

This saying also exemplifies the tides of my life. As someone who loves to plan, I've often been laughed at by the universe. And I'm trying, though perhaps not always successfully, to laugh back.

While the circumstances of my relationship with Stephen weren't unique, our story was most definitely uncommon.

From the beginning, Stephen kept reiterating that it would make a great movie, especially as the months passed and the intensity of our love and commitment grew. He had even decided which actors should play us on the big screen—Robert De Niro for him (yes, there is a very great resemblance) and Diane Keaton for me. (Really? I wonder why he thought that? Someday, I'll ask.)

I was amused and admitted I could visualize the tale—a twilight love story with a happily-ever-after ending. And perhaps our story would encourage other seniors and bring joy to adult children who feared their single parents would grow old, lonely, sad, and infirm, eventually becoming a responsibility to them.

We lightly mused over finding a screenwriter and publicist. We didn't spend serious time on the topic, but it came into conversation occasionally. What did take a more serious turn, however, was the possibility of writing the book you just read.

I had already published two books, and Stephen had written hundreds of articles, books, and chapters. My writing was emotional and practical; his was clinical and scientific. Still, we both loved to write, so the foundation was there. To add to that, we had already exchanged more than 400 emails and were continuing the stream. We had great material, and the title came to me immediately.

We agreed this book would be different from other senior love stories because it would be a "he said, she said" version of the relationship. No doubt, my romantic, feminine side would see something one way, and his perspective would be a more macho version ... or so we thought.

Section 3: Will We, or Won't We?

We decided there would be no outline ahead of time, no chapter titles to follow, no guidelines. Each of our stories would be written independently, and we had no idea what the other would say. Then we could put the pieces of the puzzle together to make a finished product.

Next came selecting an editor who would facilitate this aspect, and I was thrilled when Taylor Holland, an editor who worked on my first two books, agreed to work on this manuscript as well. She loved the approach and the topic, validating our mission. What none of us knew at that early stage was that there would be a major pivot in this wonderful plan, and the story would take a 180-degree turn.

Now there would be no happily-ever-after, no magical ending. Still, I don't regret a second of our time together. I traveled, met new and interesting people, shared the depth of another person, and learned about myself. Some of these discoveries I liked, and others disappointed me. In my mid-70s, I found someone new with whom I could share interests, truths, confidences, happiness, fear, and pain. And I think that's something special. A story worth telling.

The exciting part is that I learned, firsthand, that life and friendship don't have to cease to be thrilling because of age. Plus, I made a new friend, and as William Hazlitt once said, "There are no rules for friendship. It must be left to itself." That's exactly the path I intend to follow. Step by step.

What's next for me?

In the year since our love story began, I've vacillated between wanting to be alone (and feeling good about that), and still wanting to be in a relationship for all the reasons I outlined earlier. Who knows? Maybe one day, I'll give online dating another try.

Do I miss the male companionship? Of course, but I'm fortunate that Bob is still my good friend, and we spend time together. This is what I thought I'd have with Stephen, and I still hope that in time, perhaps I will. (Maybe next year, we'll co-author a blog telling our readers what happened. I really believe that it will be as positive, dear, and valuable as the relationship has been.)

... and so went the great plans that the universe laughed at, but I'm confident that it will have other great plans for both of us.

Authors' Letters to Each Other

Dear Stephen,

While the last pages of the book have been written, I deeply hope that it's not the final chapter in our story. Meeting you, falling in love, and sharing time and the gamut of emotions with you has been a significant part of my life story. I will cherish the memories and hope that we can continue to make new ones. Thank you for all you have shared with me and for the happiness you have brought.

As ever,

Sue

Sue

Dear Sue,

Writing this book has brought back all of the feelings and emotions we've shared. I never thought that I would find someone I could care for so deeply again, let alone online. You will always be an important part of my life. We will write new chapters in our story together. Thank you so much.

With love,

Stephen

About the Authors

SUSAN ALPERT

Susan Covell Alpert is a lecturer, author, consultant, entrepreneur, and frequent guest on radio and television shows. She founded several multi-million dollar companies and has extensive experience in the fields of negotiation, international services, travel, and business. She holds a master's degree in psychology and education from the City University of New York, Brooklyn College. Alpert resides in Newport Beach and Palm Desert, California. She is devoted to her two daughters, sons in law, and six grandchildren, and to living every day to its fullest.

STEPHEN MORSE

Stephen A. Morse, Ph.D., is a microbiologist and award-winning writer and lecturer. He has more than 47 years of experience in various aspects of microbiology, including: infectious diseases, microbial pathogenesis, antimicrobial resistance, microbial forensics, and environmental microbiology. He recently retired from the Centers for Disease Control and Prevention after having served as director of the STD Laboratory Research Program; associate director for Science, Division of Bioterrorism Preparedness and Response; and associate director for Environmental Microbiology. He has published more than 335 peer-reviewed articles, books, and chapters. Stephen has also served as an advisor to the CDC Select Agent Program, the Science and Technology Directorate for the Department of Homeland Security, and the FBI's Scientific Working Group on Microbial Genetics and Forensics.

Made in the USA
San Bernardino, CA
13 March 2019